From Arona
Nov. 8, 1990

TEXAS CHRONICLES

TEXAS
CHRONICLES

by Leon Hale

SHEARER
PUBLISHING

First published in the United States of America in 1989 by
Shearer Publishing
406 Post Oak Road
Fredericksburg, TX 78624

ISBN 0-940672-50-2   LCC 89-062901

Manufactured in the United States of America

First Edition 1989

For the Customers

CONTENTS

CONTENTS

PREFACE

Texas Chronicles is the third collection of my newspaper columns brought out by Shearer Publishing. The previous two, *A Smile from Katie Hattan* and *Easy Going*, were selections from the *Houston Post* and are still in print. This volume consists of columns chosen from my first five years at the *Houston Chronicle*. Like the first two, it is published in response to letters from readers who suggested "you ought to pick your best stuff and make a book out of it." I'm not certain these are the best but there's nothing in this collection that gives me any pain, at least not right now.

Remember that these are newspaper pieces and they appear as they ran in the paper. No attempt has been made to take the journalism out of them, so the reader will run across phrases like "next Tuesday" and "last week" in stories that may have been written four years ago. Dates when the pieces first appeared in the paper are given at the end of the book.

My thanks to the *Chronicle* for permission to reprint these columns.

—Leon Hale
August 1989

TEXAS CHRONICLES

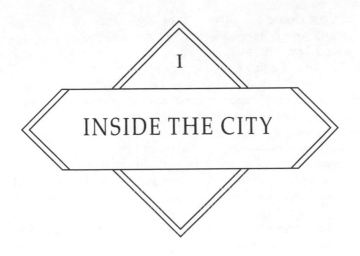

I

INSIDE THE CITY

A Country Visitor

My friend B. J. from up in Cherokee County was in town again a couple of days to get his annual checkup at the Texas Medical Center. That is the only reason B. J. will come to Houston. He is not comfortable in our city.

The first time he came to have some surgery about five years ago, he was driving a pickup. He left it at my place and rode with me, so he wouldn't have to struggle with the traffic. When we were getting in the car to go for his appointment I asked if he had locked his truck.

He said, "Why no. I don't ever lock it. I've been driving that old truck eight years and it never has been locked one time that I know of."

I convinced him it would be a good idea and he got out and tried. He came back grinning, holding up a crooked key. The lock was rusty or frozen or something and he bent the key in it. Never did get it to work.

After he'd ridden with me a couple of days he said, "Listen, I want to ease your mind. I'm not going to run off with your car and leave you afoot."

It took me a few seconds to understand that he was ribbing me about taking my keys out of the car so often. He thought it was pretty strange that I'd make a quick stop at a convenience store and run in to get a quart of milk and take my keys with me, even when he was sitting in the front seat waiting.

That's just a habit. I explained to him that parking lots of shopping centers are popular among car thieves. They don't really need keys to steal your car but it does make things a little easier for them if you leave a key in the ignition.

B. J. is amazed by all this. He said to me one time, "It must be a terrible way to live. You can't even go outside after dark without worrying that somebody's going to hit you in the head."

Do you know he's at least partly right?

I like where I live and I never worry that somebody might conk me when I go outside after dark. And yet, I'm aware all the time that I need to be watchful and I think most Houston people are that way.

If I have to walk through a parking lot at night, or along a dark street, and I see a dude sort of hanging around in the half light, I give him a wide berth because he may be up to some kind of monkey business.

But that doesn't really bother me. It's just a part of living in a city. I do not count it a terrible way to live, as B. J. said. Sometimes I not only take my keys at convenience stores but I lock the car as well, even if I'm in the store less than a minute. I do that when I see a few sleepy-eyed guys standing around out front, looking as if they don't have regular work.

The fact is that B. J. lives with a considerable stable of threats, himself, up there in East Texas in the country. But they are different dangers. He stays aware of them, just as we stay on guard in Houston against car thieves and purse snatchers and other bad citizens.

For example, when B. J. gets up in the middle of the night to go to his barn to check on a sick mare, he won't walk thirty yards outside his back door without a good light. Why? Because he doesn't want to step on a copperhead that might be lying in the grass. It happens that copperheads are plentiful on his place.

I know what he will say about copperheads.

"Being careful about snakes, that's just common sense. All you need to do is keep out of a copperhead's way."

Yeah, and it's pretty much the same way in cities with regard to thieves and muggers and the like. Being careful about them is just common sense. I know city folks who would live in 100-proof terror if they thought poisonous snakes might be lying around in their St. Augustine at night. That would disturb their sleep far more than the possibility of burglars lurking in the neighborhood. But for B. J., copperheads are simply a part of his environment.

He has the most trouble here with the traffic. He supposes that every bread truck is going to hit him. He says we do not allow enough room between cars.

I took him out Westheimer about 6:00 one time. Just before we crossed Voss I was obliged to squeeze between a city bus and a Winnebago the size of a six-room house and B. J. yelled, "##%###!" and his knuckles turned white all the way up to the elbows. He didn't think there was room enough to drive through that space.

"If I had to drive in this traffic," he said, when his blood pressure subsided, "I'd be dead in a week. It's too dangerous."

This came out of a man who has spent half a century in close company with horses. Riding them. Raising them. Breaking them. Doctoring them.

I have watched him walk among nervous horses and I felt dread, because I thought that the next second he would be kicked in the chest or knocked down and run over. And he has been hurt by horses. Thrown. Bitten. Kicked. He walks with a limp and a grunt. I never have seen the hurt leg but I'd bet a two-dollar bill it's got the imprint of a horseshoe on it.

I've never told B. J. this but I'd forty times rather drive a car out Westheimer at 5:45 p.m. with one eye shut than do what he does at home—walks up behind a horse in the corral and just stands there, within two feet of its heels, as if he's inviting the creature to boot him into paradise.

That seems to me the equivalent of driving out Westheimer without any brakes.

Good-bye to a Hotel

The morning was warm and moist. I parked on Bellefontaine just behind the Shamrock Hotel and rolled down a window and I could smell magnolia blooms.

Half a dozen others had come there to watch the great crane swing the wrecking ball and destroy the Shamrock. I didn't stay long. Nothing especially spectacular was happening. I spent a few minutes thinking what a short time it's been since that hotel was built, and now here it is being razed.

Well, wait a minute. The Shamrock opened in 1949,

right? Yes, on St. Patrick's Day. Has that been a short time? I was twenty-seven then. My son hadn't been born, and he's thirty-seven now.

Reason that seems such a short time, I remember pretty clearly the Shamrock's opening night. I was driving a 1946 two-door Ford with fog lights and white sidewall tires and bright blue seat covers and a monthly payment of $67.50.

We were living then in an apartment on Park Street, between Westheimer and Gray a few blocks east of Shepherd. I remember feeling pretty spiffy, driving that night to the Shamrock to attend the most extravagant luxury hotel opening ever held on this planet.

I went down Westheimer and turned south on Montrose Boulevard. I had washed the car and polished it and cleaned the white sidewalls and shined up the headlights and the fogs. I loved that car so. I liked to drive it real slow along Montrose and watch pedestrians study and admire it when I stopped for lights at Alabama and Richmond and Bissonnet. I supposed the pedestrians were saying, "Look, I bet they're going to the opening of the Shamrock."

Montrose was my favorite street, with its esplanade and the palms growing along it, and I grieved when they took those trees out. I still grieve about them.

According to George Fuermann's book, *Houston: Land of the Big Rich,* 150 Hollywood celebrities and 150 Texas millionaires attended the Shamrock opening, and the event was covered by 200 members of the press.

I was a member of the press at that time, sure. But I didn't really cover the event. Why? Well, because I didn't get invited.

Then why did I attend? Well, I didn't exactly *attend.* I mean I didn't go inside. What we did was park on the street and watch, the same as thousands of others who didn't get invited either.

What we hoped to see was a few of those movie stars.

I had never seen a movie star in the flesh then. The one I wanted to see the most was Dorothy Lamour. I had fallen in love with her in 1940 when she was going around in sarongs and even though I was freshly married at the time the Shamrock opened, I had still not gotten over Dorothy altogether.

She had a coast-to-coast radio show, as we called it then, on NBC. She came to Houston to originate that program in the Shamrock during the festivities. I told my bride I was interested in watching Dorothy because I admired the way she conducted her radio show. The truth was, I was hoping she'd conduct it wearing that sarong.

Anyhow, I didn't get to see her, in a sarong or out. Didn't get to see any of the other Hollywood celebrities. They all had rooms in the hotel and there was no need for them to come outdoors. If any did, we didn't get close enough to see one.

We did see the newspaper boys working the hotel entrance and they wore tuxedos.

When we got home that night the neighbors asked where we'd been and we said, "To the opening of the Shamrock, and it was sure fancy. Even the newsboys at the front door wore tuxes."

Fuermann said in his book that the Shamrock opening marked the beginning of cafe society in this town. To me it marked something else. It was a Great Event that began, for me, a new kind of life—life in a city, that is, where I'd never really lived before.

So it hasn't really been such a short time since that hotel went up. It's been thirty-eight years. I had a hard time getting used to the Shamrock its first few years, jutting up so tall and lonesome out there on that prairie. But now, when it goes I hope they build something in its place fast, because it'll sure leave a big empty space.

Won Peppy Beck?

Going out Memorial Drive I stopped at a convenience store to buy coffee and when the young lady behind the counter gave me my change she smiled nicely and said, "Won peppy beck?"

I didn't understand what she meant and had to beg her pardon. She said, "Beck, beck. Won peppy beck?" I still couldn't get what she was saying so I shrugged and nodded and said yes and went on out.

I got all the way past the Memorial Park jogging track before it hit me that she was asking if I wanted a paper bag, to put my coffee in. I suppose she thought it was peculiar that I said yes and then walked away without the bag.

I am having more and more trouble communicating in our town. You would think that the longer a guy lives in a place, the better he would understand what the people around him are saying. But for me, it's working just the opposite way.

A part of my difficulty is that so many citizens working in Houston's public places have just lately come here from other nations and they are struggling with our strange language. And I am struggling with their struggles.

I was in a service station where I bought gas on a credit card and the fellow filling out the ticket had a hard time making me understand what a river lincent is.

"River lincent, river lincent," he kept saying.

I was not familiar with that term, although it has a provocative sound and generated some interesting images. River lincent. I thought maybe it's a fish, common in the East. Or a kind of boat?

No, what it is, it's a driver's license. The young fellow finally made that clear to me, mainly by sign language. He needed to get the number off my river lincent to put on the gas ticket.

I am sorry if I seem to be complaining. I don't mean to. Learning a new language can be fun. It's just that I'm slow about it. I can get along with river lincents and peppy becks as well as the next man, if you show me a little patience.

In fact, I admire people who will attack a strange language the way some of our new citizens from the Orient and the Middle East tie into English. It takes courage.

In recent times I watched an extraordinary performance in a neighborhood icehouse. An Oriental youth came in and told a story to a little bunch of regular icehouse customers. I think the story was about a funny thing that happened when he was at work. I understood maybe every fourth or fifth word, and missed the clincher entirely. But I have to credit those icehouse folks. They laughed politely when the story ended and I don't see how they could have understood it any better than I did.

Listen, I talk pretty much the same tongue those icehouse regulars speak, but I would need to have a very, very good story before I'd get up and tell it in front of *that* audience. They can sure be harsh.

Newcomers from foreign places aren't the only Houston people I have trouble understanding. I have stood at a downtown bus stop and listened to a conversation between two young black people without quite understanding what they were talking about because they were communicating in their own dialect. And there is surely nothing foreign about those people. Probably they were born within a couple of miles of the Harris County courthouse.

My problems with understanding street talk in Houston are not new. They began back when our freeway system was being built. I noticed these strange sounds coming out of people who have to compete, when they talk, with the roar of freeway traffic. They needed to talk loud, and in short bursts.

I came to think of these people as speaking a new tongue. For a while I called it Dialect 610, because I heard it mostly around Loop 610. Sometimes I thought of it as Freeway Yap, because the sound of it put me in mind of small dogs barking at each other.

Two things about it fascinated me. One was, even though the sound was being spoken by blue-collar Texans, there was no Texas drawl in it. The other thing that interested me was, I couldn't understand it. At least not all of it.

A freeway gas station is probably the best place to hear Dialect 610. Construction workers speak it, too. And clumps of folks standing at bus stops. Here's a little sample I tried to record at a gas station that sits practically beneath a West Loop underpass:

"Boot!" That's the manager of the station yelling at one of his men working out in the service bay. I don't for a second think the fellow's name is Boot but that's how it came out of the manager. He further yapped: "You stickit 82 Cutlass?"

Boot yapped back, "No! It's a frame skin!"

"Make a thredder?"

"Yeah!"

"Stickit too!"

"Gotta metal peel!"

"Stickit anyhow!"

Now then, I have tried to spell out the sounds exactly the way they came out of those two gents. I have no idea what they were talking about. These aren't immigrants speaking. They are guys who grew up in places like Crockett and Yoakum and Giddings and Angleton.

First time I mentioned this Dialect 610 to friends, they suggested I go and have my hearing checked. But I took them then onto the street and got them to pay attention. They listened, and heard the sounds of that strange tongue, and knew not what they meant.

Maybe as this big raw town develops we are producing new dialects all along. Maybe a hundred years from now you will be roaming through a dictionary and find entries such as peppy beck, frame skin, metal peel, and river lincent.

Dawn Patrol

At this time of year there's an hour on Houston's clock that I love. It starts at ten minutes before 6:00 a.m. From then until 6:50 makes an excellent time to get out and walk.

In our neighborhood, which is just inside the West Loop between San Felipe and Woodway, we have a nice choice of places. If you want heavy woods you can go across Buffalo Bayou and walk the trails through Houston Arboretum. The forest around you is as heavy as you'll find in the Big Thicket.

But a forest of office buildings also appeals to me early in the morning. I like to walk among buildings before the people who work in them arrive. At 6:15 I enjoy going down the middle of silent business streets that'll be crowded and noisy within an hour.

The streets in our neighborhood are named for briars and hollows and oaks and ways and places, and this can be so confusing that even taxi drivers stop and ask you directions.

We've got apartments and condos but mostly we have office buildings. In the soft dawn light I walk past places where stockbrokers will soon be coming to work. Also commercial realtors. Oil people. Architects. Advertising folks. Trust and foundation officers.

The few people who are also out at this hour seem glad to see you. A fellow in a pickup cruises down Post Oak Park at 6:20 and he waves. It's like you've met him on a country road in Nacogdoches County. Just an hour later he won't wave but at 6:20 he does. Isn't that curious?

This is the hour when security guards come out of their little telephone-booth houses and stand at the curb and look along the street. Pretty soon they will be getting off duty, when all the day people arrive. Their manner seems receptive, as if they're hoping somebody to talk to will come along directly. They do have lonesome jobs.

I often walk around West Loop structures like Park Tower and the Sysco Building and do my inspection work. I count how many workers went home the night before and left their lights on. At Park Tower National Bank I generally pause and peer in the lobby and see if things are in proper order. Listen, I have an interest in that place. I supervised the construction of it, every floor of the thing, from my apartment window and I want it maintained right.

The Remington is one of my jobs, as well, there at the corner of San Felipe and Briar Oaks. My current project is supervising the new home of the Houston Junior League, just north of the Remington. I am concerned, somewhat, about that job. They seem to be putting a steel-frame roof on a wood-frame skeleton. I need to stop by during working hours and let them explain that to me. I don't know if I approve of that sort of thing.

My route is very well-established. I always walk behind the Remington so I can smell what the cooks in the kitchen are fixing for breakfast. Then I go over onto San Felipe, pause a minute in front of the doughnut shop while I talk myself out of going in and eating half a dozen plain glazed, hot out of the oven.

Sometimes there's an Event. Doesn't take much to make an Event during this hour. One is, a helicopter lands at the pad in Post Oak Park and picks up an important person who gets out of a black car that arrives at the pad about thirty seconds before the chopper lands.

I am working on who gets that kind of service. Next time I'm handy when that happens, I intend to barge up there and ask him who he is, and how come a chopper comes for him, and what he's got in that briefcase he carries. Seems to me we're entitled to know that.

Some mornings I change the route a little and go beneath the Loop and along Post Oak Boulevard. It was a country road when I came to Houston. Listen, you are talking to a dude who has been stuck in the mud of Post Oak Road. And now it's a boulevard.

On my last early-morning walk along Post Oak I came across a spotted dog at the corner of San Felipe, in front of that Hoe Hai Gai restaurant. He took up with me. We liked each other. This was a little after 6:00, when it's not easy to find a friend on the street.

He went along with me and sniffed at locked doors in the silent shopping centers. He flushed a calico alley cat in front of Tony's and chased it across the street and disappeared into the fine blue buildings of Post Oak Central. I didn't see him again.

I like the all-night supermarket at Post Oak and Westheimer. I like it best when I am the only customer in the place and the produce man has just come to work and is laying out his stuff. Good time to buy fruit. They tell me I need to eat fresh fruit. Trouble is, I will get in there and start picking out apples and oranges and peaches and cantaloupes and forget I'm afoot and buy more than I care to carry back home.

I have to watch the time. I need to be circling the Transco fountain and heading back home by 6:25. Because Houston is an early town and the magic hour is over by 6:50. After that it's not pleasant to walk.

By 7:00 drivers no longer wave at you. All they want you to do is get out of the way.

Apartment Agriculture

Christina, who is the ever-loving wife of my friend Mel, has been trying for four years to get me into potted plants. My daughter tries, as well, and so do others who believe I ought to have greenery growing around my place. They insist my premises are dull, and my air overloaded with carbon dioxide. "You need green plants," they say, "which give off oxygen."

I remember that theory from back in school but I never took it seriously because nobody ever proved to me it was true. Besides, I have known citizens to live nice long lives on nothing but concrete and asphalt without once coming up short on oxygen. Even so, I continue to be criticized for living without greenery, and sometimes friends try to get a little oxygen into my atmosphere by giving me potted plants. Christina is big about ivy, and has made me adopt six or eight little pots of it in various varieties, and they have all died. She says this is because I don't water them, and I expect she is right.

One time my daughter gave me an herb farm, which is a proposition about the size of a cigar box that sits on your kitchen drainboard. You plant in it curious things such as alfalfa seed and the seed sprouts and you can harvest the sprouts and put them in your salad. Also, I suppose, you can breathe the oxygen they give off, if you believe in that strange theory about plants.

Then I had a long looping airplane plant one time, too, and a miniature tree called a ficus growing in a big clay pot. I've still got the pot and I am using it for a wastebasket because the plant did not survive the winter of '84. The trouble with all these green things is, they require husbandry. I don't care anything about being the husband of a potted plant if it's got to be irrigated four times a week. I am not at home four times a week.

However, I have been fussed at so long about not having any tender vegatation around the house that I've taken steps. I have sprouted myself a couple of sweet potatoes, and I wish to report they are doing fine in all ways. Probably you know that you can take a sweet potato, just an ordinary yam such as you buy in the produce department, and sprout it in a jar of water. The bottom of it puts out white hairy-looking roots in the water. The top of it produces stems and leaves and these become a potato vine, which will grow all the way from the refrigerator to the living room sofa if you don't watch out.

It will grow, that is, provided you put it in the water the right way, which is tail down and eyes up. If you put the eyes down and tail up, that yam will drown. And in a few days you will begin to smell something funny in the house. What it is, it's a rotten sweet potato.

Back in my early times, sprouting sweet potatoes in this way was very popular among housewives. Nobody then had forty cents, much less fifteen bucks, to spend on a plant to grace the top of the icebox. So they sprouted yams in fruit jars. It's astonishing how much vine one potato will produce. I have seen kitchens with sweet potato vines strung along the molding and running all the way around the room at the top of the walls. I am not sure I want to live in a greenhouse of potato vines but sprouting yams does fit my circumstance. That is, I can go off for a week and the thing won't die on me from thirst, since it's got half itself down in the water.

In addition to this pair of sprouting yams I have now got two Nuevo Laredo cactuses, and I am hoping this inventory will satisfy my critics who keep wanting me to have more oxygen. A Nuevo Laredo cactus is a good plant for me because it never needs water except when rain falls in the north part of Tamaulipas, or at least that's what the fellow said who sold it to me. So I try to keep up with the weather down there, and when Nuevo Laredo gets a shower I irrigate my cactus plants and they're doing nicely. And they are very little trouble because sometimes the north part of Tamaulipas goes weeks and weeks without significant rainfall.

In one of my past lives I had a better attitude toward potted plants than I do now. Back when I was domesticated, and maintained mortgages and property taxes and lawn mowers and chinch bugs and things like that, I had an extraordinary piece of greenery that I was really fond of. It was a Mrs. Jones plant. It was given to me as a tiny green sprout by Mrs. Deacon Jones of Liberty County. I never knew the right name for that plant so I just called it Mrs. Jones and it was a wonderful plant. In summer it would get about a foot and a half tall with nice broad heart-shaped leaves. I had that same plant for almost ten years.

It never got wet from anything but pure rainwater. I kept a barrel under the downspout of the gutter and caught rainwater for Mrs. Jones. It never felt the chemical harshness of city water. I picked bugs off it and fertilized it only with earthworm castings. Along about the Fourth of July, that sweet plant would take a deep breath, strain mightily, and explode forth a magnificent pink blossom the size of my fist. People came from two and three streets away, to see my Mrs. Jones in bloom. Nobody ever was able to tell me what kind of plant it was.

I could go back to Liberty County and look for another Mrs. Jones but I don't believe I can afford to give it the attention it deserves. Right now I'll just concentrate on living in harmony with my Nuevo Laredo cactuses and sprouted sweet potatoes.

Perils in Traffic

The reason I was riding under the West Loop in a limousine is that we were on the way to a funeral. I was one of the pallbearers and we got transported to the church and then the cemetery in long black cars.

When we crossed beneath Loop 610, a young fellow in a little truck passed us on the right and saluted the limousine with an obscene gesture. Evidently he thought our driver had crowded him, or maybe the signal expressed his general feeling toward long black cars.

This was an interesting event to me. I was riding in the front seat and the limo driver said quietly, referring to the guy in the little truck, "He thinks limousine drivers aren't tough. Well, before I took this job, I did construction work."

What I think is that if circumstances had been different, if we hadn't been in a funeral procession, the limo driver would have found a way to show the fellow in the truck how construction workers react to obscene gestures.

I am astonished that so many Houston drivers feel it's perfectly safe to throw insults at other drivers in traffic. Listen, it's not safe to do that. It's not only impolite, it's dangerous.

For the last few years, shouting and fist-shaking and other demonstrations of insolence by our drivers have been increasing. This has come at a time when fuses in our town are short. When you go out on the streets, you are among people who have lost jobs, who have suffered what they see as injustice, and you mustn't imagine that they are always in a good humor.

It's long been of interest to me that Houston has the reputation as a place where you mustn't go around honking your horn. That's not because we want quiet on the street. What it says is, "If you try to drive with your horn, the way people in some cities do, you are apt to make somebody mad at you."

I always counted that a pretty good reputation for a town to have. But now I am afraid we're becoming a city of lane-switching, tailgating bird-shooters. No horns but plenty of nasty signals.

Some drivers may consider the throwing of insults from a moving vehicle to be nothing more than a way to let off steam, and that nobody is going to take them seriously.

That may be true in other large cities but it's not a safe assumption for Houston. This town isn't yet comfortable with its size, the way Chicago or New York is. Houston men, especially, deal regularly in insults but they are friendly ones, exchanged only with those we know well. We can't yet handle insults from strangers.

A couple of years ago I was pleased to get a trip to New York, and I stayed there a week, walking miles and miles in Manhattan and it was a fine experience. Dozens of little scenes return to me when I think of what Manhattan is like.

One seems pertinent here today. I was behind two fellows in business suits, walking near Times Square, and when they stepped into the street a taxi came by and turned and missed them narrowly and splashed up slush on their trousers.

One of the men let fly a really extraordinary barrage of profanity in the direction of the taxi, which had been obliged to stop just after the turn, and I felt sure the driver heard it. I thought, Hey, I may get to see a fistfight, because these are very strong words indeed.

But nothing whatever happened. The guy who launched that purple prose didn't even look to see if it had been received. He went back to talking to his companion, and seemed entirely calm once the explosion was finished. Evidently the shouting of the insults was all the satisifaction he needed.

Houston may arrive at that point some day, but it's not there yet.

If a pedestrian did that to a Houston cab driver, I believe the driver would stop and get out and walk back and serious communication would take place.

Maybe the bird-shooters I see on our streets came from other places, where a bird may be shot and nothing thought about it. Something is still thought about it here.

You will never catch me sending up offensive hand signals on Houston streets. Even if I felt like doing it, I know what would happen if I did. Two blocks later when I got caught by a red light, some huge person with fiery breath and fierce eyes would walk up to my car and ask me to step out and talk. I don't need that.

◆———————————◆

A Small Relative

A small relative of mine, not yet six, is visiting from the Deep South. His home is in a small town in Alabama, and I thought while he was here I would expose him to the wonders of the big city.

He has not been easy to impress. He studied our tall buildings and our squirting fountains and nodded politely. He made muffled noises that seemed to express approval, but I wasn't sure. I have never been certain how to interpet the sounds of people this size.

I learned he had never seen a major league baseball game, much less one played indoors, so we organized an expedition to watch the Astros play the Chicago Cubs. My guest indicated this seemed worthwhile and fished a baseball glove out of his suitcase. Said he'd catch a foul ball for a souvenir.

One of my theories about Houston is that no person, no matter how sophisticated, can fail to be impressed the first time he walks in and looks down at the playing field of the Astrodome. But I wasn't sure how the sight struck my visitor. He studied the place with what appeared to be respect. He kept a solemn face. He made no remark.

He did take a picture. He carries a camera and is always on the watch for something to shoot. His father, also a relative of mine, says the kid won't photograph what he doesn't like. This camera is the kind that spits out instant prints, and film for it is costly, so its operator is tight as wallpaper about popping the shutter. I supposed this meant he thought the Astrodome was an acceptable wonder.

By some miracle, our seats for the ball game were superior. We were on the second row, exactly behind the home-plate end of the Houston dugout. When the Astros emerged to bat, we could have stood up and shaken hands if they had not been busy with other matters.

To me this was an extraordinary privilege, as I am accustomed to sitting in cheaper seats where I need field glasses to read the names on the players' shirts.

My small guest was not impressed. He seemed mildly annoyed that he wasn't on the front row instead of the second, so he could get a clear shot at a foul ball. I tried to explain to him that the only person in the Dome who had a better shot at a foul ball was Alan Ashby. Who was catching Bob Knepper. Who was pitching.

I also explained that he wasn't going to catch a foul. I was clear on that point. I told him I have been going to baseball games ever since the discovery of America, and I have never once sat in the stands and gotten a souvenir baseball.

That didn't capture this attention. I'm not sure he even

heard me. And in the bottom of the third inning, he had a baseball.

I didn't see exactly how it happened. But I believe a man in the first row, who seemed to know everybody on the team, caused a ball to appear and it ended up in the glove of my small relative, and this pleased him. I don't know that he was surprised. He did grin a little.

I made a fine speech about the scoreboard and how it erupted when an Astro hit a home run. How the cowboys shot off their pistols. How the bull roared and charged across the sky.

Nobody on our side hit a home run, but the Astros won the game and the scoreboard lighted up, and my little relative stood in his seat and took a picture of it and we went home.

Next morning, he got up and said to me, "Let's see what's on TV."

He knew how to operate the remote control and how to get cable stations I wasn't aware of. We sat and watched terrible wonders, on cartoon television.

Earthquakes that made the planet heave. Tidal waves that washed great cities away and tossed ocean liners far inland.

We saw things from dreamed-of worlds. Creatures with awful mouths that swallowed spaceships. We saw cars that talked. Robots with lightning in their metal hands. Giant monsters with arms that curled and grasped victims across entire states.

So then I understood why this little person cannot be much impressed with the ordinary marvels of our city. He is a child of television, and in his five years he has seen in his own home more wonders than his grandfather can imagine.

I try to think what this tiny person, so dear to me, will find in the world that will thrill or impress or frighten him.

The "Dallas" Problem

It was a quiet evening and we were staying home, reading and trying to recover from a flu-bug attack. She looked up from a magazine and said, "In France (she might have said Italy, I don't know, or Germany), people form their images of Texans from 'Dallas,' the TV show. What do you think of that?"

Told her I was opposed to the idea. Because I could tell from her tone that she wanted me to oppose it.

"Well, it really disturbs me," she said. "Doesn't it disturb you that people all over the world think Texans are like those awful characters on that TV show?"

It might disturb me more, I said, if I had ever watched "Dallas," but I never have.

We went back to reading then and presently she said, "What did you say, just a moment ago, about watching 'Dallas'?"

That I never have.

"Not ever?"

That's right. I've seen little bits of it, like when somebody was running through the channels, looking for football games or good old movies.

"But you've never watched an episode all the way through?"

Correct. Never have.

"That's extraordinary," she said, and looked at me with fresh interest, or something. "You may be the only adult American who's never watched 'Dallas.'"

Is that bad?

"Well, yes, in a sense it is. Whether you think the show is good or bad, it's a significant part of our culture and you ought to be aware of it." She looked at the clock. "Hey, it's coming on in about twenty minutes. Would you watch it?"

Well, okay, I guess.

"You ought to stay with it, just this once, all the way through, all right?"

So I said I would. At the top of the hour she switched on the TV and a lot of preliminary scenes rolled by.

"That's J. R.," she said. "You *do* know J. R. Ewing, don't you?"

Sure I do, but I thought he was dead.

"Why did you think that?"

Because he got shot, I know that. All last summer everybody was going around asking "Who shot J. R.?"

She whooped. "Last *summer*? You know how long ago J. R. was shot? Years and years. I don't know *how* long."

He didn't die?

"He didn't die," she said. "That's Bobby Ewing, J. R.'s younger brother, the one in jeans and the sport coat. He did die, but he came back."

Hey, I said, that's not a bad image to project to the people of the world—that Texans can die and be resurrected even before the Judgment Day.

"Don't be smarty-pants. Try to get something out of this."

A love scene was happening on the screen. "That's Sue Ellen, J. R.'s wife, with one of her lovers, Nicholas. He's the only Yankee I ever saw on this show."

Maybe she's exhausted the domestic supply and has begun importation.

"That's Cliff Barnes," she said, ignoring my previous comment, which I thought was pretty good. "Barnes is J. R.'s enemy. There's a lot of really nasty people in this. It's greed city."

I had trouble keeping up. There'd be quick little scenes. An old man trying to court a young girl. A father promising his young son that nobody would ever steal him (the son) away. Was that Bobby saying that? A pretty lady coming to J. R. and trying to strike a business deal and he ends up pretty near raping her before our very eyes, and when he gets home he is obliged to explain that he had to work late. Ho ho ho.

"There's J. R.'s diabolical grin," said my interpreter. "He's made a fortune out of that. You have to have J. R. on this show. People enjoy watching him operate."

I complained about the scenes being so short and disconnected that I couldn't get any sense of an ongoing story and she said, "It's complex. So much happening. I think that's what's kept the show going. People develop an interest in the characters and care about them."

Maybe so. Toward the end of the show I got interested in J. R., who was attacked by his little brother, Bobby, and they had this fight and fell into the swimming pool and the last I saw, Bobby was holding his big brother's head underwater and inviting him to drown.

I'm confident that J. R. will surface, gasping but healthy, and we will present to the world the suggestion that Texans can hold our breath underwater for a week.

The Skewed Image

The last few weeks I have done a lot of talking to strangers, mainly about Texas. This was because I spent time in places like Boston and Chicago, and in a couple of provinces in Canada. Also, I rode on several airplanes and sat beside and talked to citizens from various far-flung locations, including England.

Abigail Worthington. That's a name in my notebook. I sat beside her on a plane ride out of Boston to Chicago.

She was born and grew up in London and she looks exactly as you would expect somebody named Abigail Worthington to look. She was on her way to Cedar Rapids, Iowa, to see her grandchildren.

"Tell me about Houston," she said.

Have you ever been obliged to describe the city you live in to a person who has never seen it? It's a pretty tough assignment because your audience will expect the description to be brief and concise. If you stutter, or hesitate, or qualify, they will begin to doubt that you live where you say you live. Houstonians probably ought to practice giving descriptions of this town, in twenty-five words or less, before they travel to other parts of the world and start meeting Abigail Worthingtons out of London.

A traveling Texan is almost certain to be asked about the state. People everywhere have always been interested in Texas. I remember getting surprised about that, the first time I ever left the state and went anywhere farther away than Reynosa.

In the army I bunked a good while next to a little guy named Fred Irwin who came from Pennsylvania. We would go into town and meet strangers and they would say, "Tell me about Texas. Do you live on a ranch?"

Irwin said to me one night, "Nobody ever asks me to tell them about Pennsylvania. They always want to know about Texas. Why is that?" I didn't know why. I don't know now, either.

They still ask if you live on a ranch. To the Texans who do live on ranches, it must be a great satisfaction to answer that question. To say, "Yes, we live on thirty-two sections just west of the Pecos River in Terrell County."

Then the party from New Jersey, who is doing the asking, will want to know how much land a section is. The ranch person can explain modestly that it's 640 acres, a square mile. That's got to be fun, to say that and watch the eyebrows rise.

One time in 1972, I went up to Chicago and in O'Hare Airport I met a lady who was interested in Texas. She asked, "Where do you live?"

I already knew what that meant. It could be translated into, "Do you live on a ranch?" I told her where. She wanted to know how big it was. She didn't say so but she meant, "How much land?"

I told her it was two-thirds of an acre, with a three-bedroom FHA house and five post oak trees and a pair of mimosas that I bought at the nursery for $3.50 each plus sales tax. I told her my monthly payment was $87.62 and my taxes were $230 a year and I was hoping in desperation that I would be able to meet those obligations and support a wife and a couple of kids.

She was destroyed by that answer. The state of Texas was destroyed along with it, in that lady's head. I have always regretted doing that.

So I don't do it any longer.

Nobody wants the truth about Texas. It doesn't fit what they think about us. I don't tell them that I can't ride a horse. I make vague remarks instead, about horses. I say, "I have fallen off some of the best horses in Texas."

They like that. To them it means that I have tried to ride bucking broncos. When what it really means is, any time I got on a good cowhorse I fell off. Which is the pure-dee truth.

The image of Texas is concreted into the heads of people living far away from us. It's a state, to them, of ranches and oil fields, nothing more. Houston, especially, has gotten a great lot of exposure in national magazines. But the mass of people don't read magazines. What they do is watch TV. So that Texas to them is "Dallas," the soap opera.

In Newfoundland, Canada, I was introduced to a boy of ten by his parents. A really handsome young fellow. He grinned at me and said, "J. R." Then he said, "Sue Ellen."

I did understand that he was naming characters out of "Dallas" but it took me a minute to see what he was telling me. He was saying, "I watch TV so I know about Texas."

What are you going to do about that? Are you going to say: "Look, young man, that TV show is outrageous fiction. It reflects almost zero about the lives of Texas people. The script is probably written by talented folks from Vermont or somewhere. If you walked through downtown Dallas, you would keep walking thirty years before you found anybody whose life was the same as J. R.'s."

Are you going to tell him: "Even in Houston, which is forty times the oil town Dallas is, you'll find very few folks like those on that TV show. You could go all the way across Houston, from any direction, surveying citizens you met along the streets, and you'd come across maybe one out of a hundred people who could draw you a reasonable sketch of what a drilling bit looks like, or tell you why it takes a derrick to get oil out of the ground."

As for ranching: A great majority of Texans have never been inside the gates of a working ranch, and don't know the difference between a heifer and a herd bull. But you can't tell that to citizens of Boston or Chicago. They know better, from watching TV.

◆————————————————————————◆

Games without Supervision

Several old apartment buildings in my neighborhood were torn down recently and the job took a long time because the contractor did the work with care so he could save and sell useful materials.

For several weeks, men in pickups would come to that site late in the afternoon to buy and haul away stuff that had been in those buildings. They carried away doors, picture windows, kitchen cabinets, light fixtures, bathtubs, lumber, bricks.

These were men who know the value of things that might seem old and useless to most of us, and I liked watching that and seeing materials rescued.

Half a dozen schoolboys who live nearby were also interested. I saw them almost every day there, milling around, watching the buildings come down, waiting for the bulldozers that would come and do the final work.

I went out of town two or three days and missed the dozers. When I got back the buildings were gone, the rubble removed, and the property nicely leveled. And there were the six schoolboys, playing ball on the vacant property where the apartments had stood.

They must have trotted onto that lot and started the game the minute the last truck left. Something about that gave me the grins. In the middle of a great city, if you clear a little space, boys will appear and begin playing ball on it.

These are not boys out of privileged families. They don't wear fifty-dollar sneakers. For a bat they used what looked to me like the handle off a shovel, and they were swinging at a green tennis ball.

Somehow I have developed more than a casual interest in the games children play when they are not supervised. They often show imagination and creativity.

Not just city kids, either. The country ones are the same way.

One day I was loafing along south on U.S. 59, down close to the Fort Bend–Wharton county line, and these young black boys had a basketball game going in a pasture beside the highway. They had nailed their goal up on a full-sized billboard standing just inside the fence.

The biggest and best backboard in the West, folks, one that wouldn't come apart or warp or lean over or fall down.

I had to fight the yearning to get out and shoot a couple of baskets with those kids, and try to bank a hook shot off the billboard for two points.

But boys don't want old gray-headed dudes messing in their games. They need to be left alone.

That sort of thing, rigging a goal on a signboard, makes me remember the first basketball game I was ever in. It was on Grandma Hale's farm at hog-killing time. When the men butchered a hog they would take its bladder out and we'd wash it good and blow it up and tie it like a balloon and it made an excuse for a ball.

We cut the bottom out of a rusty lard can and nailed it on the side of the barn for a goal and shot baskets with that pig bladder, which was about the size of a volleyball. Our need for games was that strong.

I'm afraid the need fades slowly. The other day I wanted to get out and ask for a turn at bat on that vacant lot the bulldozers had cleared. I've had experience in such a game. Just one more time I'd like to know the feeling you get when you hit a tennis ball with a sturdy stick. If you catch it solid, man, it flies a mile.

I sometimes wonder if children would be happier if we quit organizing their games for them. Maybe they would go back to playing jacks, or hopscotch. Maybe they'd make kites and fly them.

They might make stilts. I haven't seen a kid on stilts in many years. I bet we have people in college in this town who've never made a stilt, or even seen one, or understand one.

They might begin creating fine games to play with old car tires, the way their grandparents did. We used to have boys gather from miles distant on the top of a rise to see who could roll his tire downhill the farthest, and the only prize to the fellow who won was sweet recognition that he was the winner. And that was plenty.

There was no equipment that cost $100 at the sporting goods store. No trophies awarded. And no adults were involved.

If they asked you when you got home what you'd been doing, you just said, "Nothin'."

Not Quite Kissing

The last few years I have been having trouble with a social custom practiced in this town. It is called kissing but that's not what it is. Cheeking, is what I call it. A man sees a woman friend he hasn't seen in two or three weeks, he is entitled to put the side of his jaw up against her face, so that for a split second they are in cheek-to-cheek contact.

The instant skin touches skin, both parties make a little smooch sound with their mouths. It's not a kiss. They simply open their mouths a little and then shut them back up, similar to the way fish do all the time.

Most cheeking is done man to woman. What I mean, you don't see many men doing it to other men. Women are often seen cheeking other women but I don't think they enjoy it much.

I don't mean to sound critical of this custom. In fact, I sort of like it but I do think we need some rules set forth. I am fairly new in the field of cheeking and I need guidelines.

For instance, I'd like to know when I am supposed to cheek a lady and when I am not supposed to. Nobody can tell me. So I am just blundering along, writing my own laws of cheeking, based on personal experience and observation.

It's clear that a guy is not entitled to cheek a lady the

first time he meets her. Even if he's known her husband forty years, worked in the same office, fought in the same war, he must not cheek her on first meeting.

I don't believe cheeking can properly begin until the fourth meeting. Not even then, unless cheekers have gotten along especially well on the previous three occasions. But that law is underdeveloped. It's been conceived, in my mind, but not really born yet.

Then we have the question of frequency. If a man and a woman meet at the tailor shop and haven't seen one another for three weeks, okay, they can cheek. But if they happen to meet the same afternoon at the grocery store, they mustn't do it again.

Say a man and a woman work together in an office. They mustn't cheek daily. Office cheeking is not proper. However—and this is passing strange—if these two chance to meet in the evening, say at a restaurant, they may cheek freely, even though they have been working side by side all day. It has something to do with the coincidence of the meeting. This rule is still foggy to me.

But what gives me the most trouble is the actual execution of the cheek. I have looked in books on social behavior and I have found no help.

On which side do women wish to be cheeked? There is need for a public understanding on this question, the same as we all understand which side of the street to drive on.

In the beginning I assumed that the thing to do was bear to the right, and aim for contact on the left side of the lady's face.

However, this doesn't always work. I meet women who evidently wish to be cheeked on the right side. Maybe they are left-handed. Others don't seem to prefer one side over the other and this can produce awkwardness. Sometimes you see a couple ducking and dodging and switching directions, looking for an agreement on how to get the maneuver going, and they end up bumping noses and that spoils everything.

This greeting has got to be done with grace or it's not a success.

One thing for certain, a guy must be prepared to change his approach on short notice. Here's an example: You start to do a customary cheek, and you're confronted with a new hair style, one that may hide the entire side of the face that you intended to go for.

To deal with this frustration I use what I call the air cheek, adopted from the basketball term which means the ball was shot and didn't hit the rim, net, or backboard. Doing the air cheek, you don't touch anything. You just lean in and make a quick pass with your jaw and call it a job done.

Women's hats are coming back now and that's another problem. I went up against a new challenge the other day—a friend wearing a hat with a great straw brim that turned sort of down in front. Such hats could destroy the entire cheeking custom.

I saw there wasn't any way for me to work up under that hat and get at her. So I just shook her hand.

Life beneath the Sink

The other afternoon I got back from a short trip out of town and when I went in the front door I heard these squeaky little voices coming from beneath my kitchen sink. I opened the cabinet door just a crack and looked in and saw exactly what I expected—a meeting of the cockroaches who live in my apartment.

Evidently the entire colony was present because I have never before seen such a congregation of bugs. The Head

Roach was addressing the membership. He had leaned back on his haunches, waving his feelers and forelegs as he spoke. He was using a box of SOS pads for a rostrum.

" . . . and so I can't heap sufficient praise on our leadership," the Head Roach was saying. "This has been by far the best year the colony has had since we occupied these premises. Our numbers have increased threefold, our immunization program is progressing, and the old dude we're living with is showing signs of surrender. He hasn't bought a new can of roach-killer in six months. Let me repeat, do not waver in your purpose. Eventually we'll wear him down, he'll quit fighting us, and the place will be ours."

He cleared his throat importantly. "Now then," Head Roach went on, "I want a report on the immunization program. J. B.? How are we fixed for supply?"

A very old roach raised his head to respond. The tips of his feelers are almost solid white. He has been around my place a long time. In the colony he is distinguished for having developed a total immunity to the active ingredients in five leading brands of roach poison. A year ago the Head Roach put him in charge of immunization for the colony.

He speaks: "We've never been in better shape, supplywise, H. R. I've now got on hand two full cc's of the straight stuff out of this spray can he's currently using. We've never had that much available before."

H. R. raises his feelers in surprise. "Fantastic, J. B. How did you ever get that much?"

"From his wet sponges, H. R.," said the ancient bug. "You know his habits. He'll come into the kitchen and get mad at us and squirt that spray can all over the drainboard. Then he'll get worried that he's going to poison himself and he'll wet those sponges and wipe the stuff up. Fortunately he leaves the sponges on the back of the sink. Our lab people down in the drainpipes figured a way to isolate the active ingredients trapped in the sponges. Then we simply collected and stored them."

Head Roach was pleased. He said: "You mean you have extracted from his sponges a supply of pure phenol methyl-carbamate?"

"Right," the old roach said. "Dichloro vinyl dimethyl phosphate, as well. I am talking straight stuff, H. R. No petroleum distillate. Do you know what this means? Hopefully, at this point in time, we'll be able to initiate primary immunization to every juvenile in the colony. I'm optimistic that within six months we'll have every one of our little bitty roaches eating that stuff for breakfast and asking for seconds."

A tinny cheer went up from the audience when the old roach lowered his head and sank back into his thoughts.

"I think that about covers it," said Head Roach from the SOS box, "unless anybody has an announcement."

A wiry young bug in the back spoke up. "Sir, I'd like to say a couple of words about our Attack and Contaminate Force."

"Come forward," said Head Roach. The young bug went forward. He said, "I just want to say that we have two openings on the Attack and Contaminate Force, or the A.C.F. as most of us know it. A.C.F. is a volunteer group, and volunteers can report to me in the grease trap. Thank you, sir."

Head Roach said, "Hold on, son. Why don't you give a brief account of what A.C.F. does? Some of these newer roaches may not be fully aware of your contribution."

The young bug returned to the SOS carton. "The A.C.F.," he said, "is a highly trained force of young adult roaches. What we look for in a volunteer is speed and agility and, of course, spirit. Most of us are male, but in recent times we have been accepting female applications because we've recognized that some girl roaches are as fast and agile as boy roaches.

"What we do, we hide in the kitchen when the person comes to fix a meal. Say he puts down a slice of bread on his butcher block, and turns to the refrigerator to get the mayonnaise. On signal we dart out and hop on the bread and run around and around on it. We have to keep doing that until he sees us. Then we dash away and hide, most times in the dishwasher.

"He'll think the bread is contaminated with disease organisms from our feet, and he'll pitch it in the garbage sack where we can eat it at our leisure during the night. A significant portion of the total food supply of the colony is provided by A.C.F. activity."

Cheers went up. Feet stomped. Antennae waved.

"For example," the young roach said in conclusion, "last week's pepperoni pizza banquet came to you as the result of an A.C.F. raid. I thank you."

More cheers.

While they were distracted I thought I could wipe them out. I whipped open the cabinet door and let fly an awful fog of roach poison. But they were too quick for me. Out of that large gathering of roaches, only a couple of them flopped over on their backs and kicked. My guess is even those two were putting on an act. Probably when I shut the door they hopped up and went laughing off into the plumbing somewhere.

Spring Harvest

This year the cedar waxwings harvested the pyracantha berries on the first day of March at two o'clock in the afternoon. That noisy event is one of my personal indicators that spring has come to Houston.

Another indicator is the soft bubbly music of purple martins, soaring high over the neighborhood early in the morning. I first heard that five days after the waxwings stripped the pyracantha. Usually the two signs occur within a week of one another that way.

A third indicator I watch for is the first sprig of lime green on the hackberry just outside the windows near this desk. Those dinky little leaves are the color of spring to me. Not the dark green of summer but a cool lime. This is the only time hackberry leaves are very pretty. Well, wait, I like them also in the fall when they turn yellow and twist loose from their twigs and go down in a perfect flutter, each one rotating at exactly the same rate. That's nice to watch.

The harvest of the pyracantha berries is more fun, though, and creates an extraordinary racket.

My bush and tree book says the narrow-leaf firethorn, or *pyracantha angustifolia,* sometimes makes a tree twenty feet tall. The one I can see out my front door is that big, I think. All winter it has been drooping with the weight of a high crop of fruit.

When February fades and the northers start playing out before they reach us, I like to keep my door open and listen for the cedar waxwings. Because they stop here several times late in February to check the ripeness of those pyracantha berries.

You can tell when they stop because of the high-pitched note they make. Almost a squeak. In fact, sometimes I get fooled by a squeaky wheel on a grocery cart that a lady pushes along our street a couple of days a week. Sounds a lot like a cedar waxwing.

The waxwings won't eat a berry until it gets to a certain stage of maturity known only, I suppose, to birds. I wonder how they know when that stage arrives. I have watched and I can't see them testing. They come to check, but I have never seen one pecking at a berry and rejecting it as not quite ready. I suspect they judge by smell. Or maybe they can tell by looking.

They come in flights of fifteen to twenty birds, and they always settle into the top of the great sycamore to the left of my front door. They sit up there squeaking at one another, looking down at the pyracantha. They stay a couple of minutes and if the berries aren't ready they fly off.

Then one day they return, as they did on March 1, and the berries are just right and the harvest takes place. It's something worth watching. In the case of this particular firethorn, the harvest lasts about as long as a basketball game. You need to be on time or you'll miss everything.

The day of the feast, the waxwings come not in small flights but by the hundreds. I decided on 500 birds this year. They're not easy to count so that's an estimate. The air around here was just one big squeak.

A curious thing is, they harvested that tree in what seemed to be a prearranged and understood procedure. They didn't all eat at once. They sat in the top of the sycamore and flew down in an orderly stream, as if in turn. A constant stream of whirring feathers. They formed a column of cedar waxwings, less than a foot in diameter. Half the column was descending, the other half going back up, at a forty-five-degree angle from the top of the sycamore to the tree of berries.

Do you imagine that every bird understood how long it was entitled to stay in the pyracantha and eat? Or did every one stay until its craw was stuffed, and then clear out of the way to make room for another? No way to tell, but it was plain that each bird got seconds and thirds and fourths, and maybe tenths and twelfths.

The harvest was not without conflict and competition. A cedar waxwing isn't the only bird that knows what day a pyracantha berry is ready to eat. We have a resident mockingbird here who isn't yet married for the season, so it's alone and hates cedar waxwings and it loves ripe pyracantha berries. It attended the harvest and fought and lost.

Cedar waxwings know how to make a feathered fool out of a mockingbird. They depend on the mockingbird's greed. The mockingbird has been waiting all winter for those berries to ripen and whetting his beak for the big day. Then when that day came, enter all those outsider waxwings.

If the mockingbird had perched quietly on one branch and eaten, and ignored the outsiders, it would have gotten a share of the harvest. But it would not. It flapped around the whole time, trying to spook 500 cedar waxwings out of the tree. They paid no attention. And when they departed, the berries were gone and the mockingbird was exhausted. I don't believe it got one berry. Mockingbirds are good singers but they're dumb about a lot of things.

Before the coming of the waxwings, that tree was solid red with ripe berries. Two hours later, when they left, I went out there and looked the best I could and I didn't find one red berry on the tree.

The only thing left was one limp mockingbird, looking empty and frustrated. A victim of his own greed.

A River to Think About

It was about 12:30 p.m. on a gray moody day and I was sitting in a drugstore booth, eating a hamburger and thinking about the James River out in Mason County. I am getting lonesome for that sweet stream.

A fellow I'd never met came up and said all the seats were taken during the lunch rush and would I mind if he sat across from me in the booth and ate a hamburger. I said I wouldn't mind, which I didn't, even though I was having an entirely satisfactory lunch, sitting here thinking about the river. I got on with my thinking, and pretty soon he said, "You're the one who writes stories for the paper, aren't you?"

Told him I am one of the ones who do. We've got hundreds of them here in town.

"I'm sorry to say I never have read it much," he said, referring to my contribution to the paper. "I don't have a lot of time to read. I get around to sports and the funnies, and that's about it. I just don't have time."

Told him no need to apologize for not reading my stuff. There are many thousands who don't read it. I said I understood the time problem. I don't have time myself to watch TV much. When his hamburger came, he asked for ketchup to put on it. When a guy past the age of forty puts ketchup on a hamburger, I get cautious toward him. This is one of my eccentricities. I would not, for example, invite a guy to go with me to the James River if I knew he put ketchup on hamburgers.

"I'm not a writer," he said, chewing on his ketchupy burger. "I've tried it some but I'm just not a writer."

I assured him that it's all right not to be a writer and

he said: "I've always wondered how you know what to write about. Do you sit around thinking of things that would make subjects?"

Well, yes, I suppose it's fair to say that. You do sit around thinking of things a lot of the time.

"That's interesting," he said. "How about right now? Were you thinking of something when I sat down here?"

Yes.

"What was it? Do you mind saying what it was?"

The James River.

"The James River. Isn't that in Canada?"

No, it's in Mason County out the other side of Austin.

"I'm not too familiar with that part of the state," he said. "The James River. Is it a good place to fish?"

I said it's my favorite place to fish in this state.

"I go mostly to Lake Livingston, and Toledo Bend sometimes," he said. "I've got a bass boat I trail up there. Last spring, in June, friend of mine and I filled two big Igloos with bass and white perch, in one weekend at Toledo. Just about stocked our freezers."

We had silence for a short time. Then he said, "The James River. Do you slaughter 'em out there?"

No. I have never brought home any fish in an icebox from the James.

"But you were sitting here thinking about it," he said. "What were you thinking about it?"

I decided not to tell because I didn't believe I could get across to him why I liked sitting in a drugstore off the West Loop and thinking about a rocky stream two hours west of Austin. It has to do with fish but not in a bass-boat way. Not in a way that has a relationship to filling iceboxes or stocking freezers.

I was thinking, hoping, that some good things are happening right now in what we call the canyon.

Twice a year I go with friends to the James, and we

camp on the bank and fish a little and cook stew and beans and fry what we catch, and we talk about all the things in the world that matter to us.

A short walk upstream from where we camp, there's the mouth of a canyon I am in love with. In times of normal rain, the canyon has rock-bottomed pools where bream and black bass swirl. The canyon walls are lined with scrub timber that makes excellent cover for wild turkey, bobcats, whitetail deer, raccoons, skunks, opossums, squirrels. Sometimes the turkeys fly over the canyon in a formation that the air force ought to study. I go to church on these natural wonders.

Last spring the canyon was asleep. It needed rain, and little had fallen for a year. The fishing holes had dried up. We walked over rocks where we had caught black bass the previous season. It was sad.

But since that time, rains have come. When the city gets dreary like this, I enjoy thinking about the James River (a tributary of the Llano) running high and rusty. So that the black bass and the catfish and the bream ran up into the canyon to escape the sediment. I can see them waiting, almost still, in gravel beds and beneath rocks, until the storms and floods were finished.

Then when the flood receded, they were trapped in the high pools where the water is becoming pure and green, and they will be there, hungry, when we go back in the spring. April. We'll go back in April.

He asked, there in the drugstore booth, "How big a bass have you caught out there in the James River?"

About a pound and a half, I said.

He caught himself and didn't laugh. But he said that last spring he had got up at 4:00 a.m. on Toledo and caught sixteen pounds of black bass and was back in the motel, eating bacon and eggs, by 7:30.

I believe he felt a little sorry for me.

Bushy-Tailed Rodents

For the past two weeks I have been having daily water fights with a squirrel.

I know this seems undignified and I certainly didn't intend to mention it here. But a couple of my neighbors saw me trying to dash a quart of water on the squirrel and probably they figure I have gone off the edge. So I had better explain this activity, in defense of my reputation as a fairly sane citizen.

What started the trouble with the squirrel was the baby mockingbird.

About fifty feet from where I sit when I type this stuff, a pair of mockingbirds is struggling to raise a family. They started out with four babies and have two left, which is not bad considering how many boar cats we've got slinking around the premises.

Well, I am in favor of mockingbirds and I started trying to help this family on groceries. Mockingbirds don't care for the sunflower seed I put out for the cardinals but they like fruit. I had two or three tired apples in the kitchen so I cut one up and put it out on my patio, on top of the whiskey barrel I use for a bird feeder.

First time I ever had mockingbirds on my feeder. They loved that apple.

Soon as the baby birds could fly, their parents brought them to my barrel and taught them how to eat apples. Two young mockingbirds, full feathered but still with the speckled breasts they'll later lose, have got huge appetites. They are both bigger now than their parents, who have lost weight keeping the children fed.

In fact, those adult birds are reduced to nothing but

skin, bone, and feathers, and I know they'll be relieved when the babies get grown and leave home. So will I, because I've been buying apples for them now for two weeks.

I discovered I was also buying apples for this pot-bellied squirrel that started coming to the barrel. It would chase away the birds and sit there and eat twenty cents worth of fruit before I'd ever see it.

So I began running it off, and pretty soon it grew to hate me. I wasn't in love with it, either. We went to war, and we're still fighting.

I think probably it's a mistake to start buying apples for baby mockingbirds. Without my interference, their parents would raise them on bugs and help reduce Houston's booming insect population. But once I began, I hated to stop the feeding.

When the apple is eaten from the barrel, do you think those birds fly off and start hunting worms and grasshoppers and berries the way they're supposed to? They do not. They sit on the fence and complain, and wait for me to go to the store for more apples.

So I don't want to be wasting apples on a squirrel, which is already overweight anyway.

When I chase it off the barrel, that creature stops just out of range of my broom and stares at me and gives off a shameful barrage of cuss words. This is one profane animal.

Maybe you are a fan of squirrels. Not me. I used to think they were cute but I don't anymore. They're hateful. Look in a squirrel's eyes. You will find nothing there but hostility, even while you are feeding it.

Remember a squirrel is a rodent. Shave all the fur off its tail and you know what you would have? Nothing but a big old long-tailed rat.

If we started calling a squirrel what it really is, a bush-tailed rodent, not so many people would think it's such a nice animal.

I began plotting dirty tricks against this squirrel, and I did it with a perfectly comfortable conscience. I put half a dozen empty aluminum cans in a small plastic garbage sack and tied it with a string. Then I put a cup hook in the overhang of my upstairs neighbor's balcony, so that I could suspend the sack of cans exactly above my barrel. I ran the string into my apartment, to make a little booby trap controlled from my living room.

When the squirrel got to eating the apple, I would release the string and down would come the sack on the barrel. This was really satisfying. Once I bombed that rodent square across its rump. The cans weren't heavy enough to hurt, but they made a wonderful racket and the squirrel jumped about a yard high. It sailed off the patio and disappeared. In a minute it poked its ratty nose and hostile eyes back over the fence and looked around and asked, "What in Harris County was *that*?"

I believe eventually the booby trap would have run the thing out of the neighborhood but the noise also scared the birds off so I had to retire it. Now I fight with water.

This squirrel despises water. When I can give it a thorough dousing, it doesn't come back for twenty-four hours. I don't mind saying I've developed a good deal of skill at wetting squirrels down. It requires sneaking up with a quart jar of water and then throwing quick and leading the target just right, like a quarterback leading a tight end on a short pass over the middle.

My battle plan is to keep that squirrel wet as possible. I am at work now on rigging a better water trick, one that will deliver a full gallon at once and wash away any taste that rodent ever had for store-bought apples. This is kin to the stunt college boys used to play, when they'd rig a pail of water over a dormitory door so that the water would spill on the next person who came into the room. I feel there is no reason this would not work on squirrels.

I believe I am winning.

II

TIMES PAST

Daring the Devil

Back in my old hometown long ago, when the carnivals came through, sometimes they would have daredevils who earned their money in hard ways, performing death-defying stunts to thrill the local folks. A daredevil would walk a high wire without a net below, or drive a motorcycle through a flaming wall. Or he would dive into a shallow tank of water from a high place.

I haven't seen a carnival tank diver perform in many years, but I suppose somewhere in the world they still do. I see things frequently to remind me of them. The metal water tanks for livestock that stand near windmills are similar to the tanks that the daredevils would leap into.

The big plastic swimming pools common now in back-yards—I never see one without thinking of the tank divers and how they thrilled us. I thought of them recently when I heard about the fellow who would get inside a barrel and drop from the roof of the Astrodome into a water tank. As you probably know, when the stunt was attempted, the barrel hit the rim of the tank, and the man was killed.

That fellow was more than a carnival tank diver. He was one of the Niagara Falls barrel men, but the old tank divers were cut out of the same cloth. Men who were somehow driven to risk their lives for—well, for what? Money? Applause? The thrill of stunts?

When a carnival would come to town, we used to hang around while they were setting up, and watch, and hope to get a little work carrying water or running errands. The best prospect was we might get a chance to talk to the daredevil.

The daredevils on television now don't look anything like the ones I remember seeing in the flesh.

One time I ran an errand for a fellow who was helping to erect a tower, while a carnival was setting up in our town. The tower was for the daredevil, the star of the show. The story in the paper said that the daredevil could climb that tower and dive into a very small tank, and the water in the tank would be burning.

That sort of thing generated a lot of enthusiasm around our town. We would talk about it for several days in advance of the show. We tried to act as if we weren't especially interested, but we didn't fool anybody. A guy would say: "Big deal, jumpin' into a water tank. Who cares?" But the very guy who said such a thing would be standing in the front tier of spectators when the daredevil climbed the tower.

The fellow helping erect the tower that time sent me to the store for a pack of cigarettes. He was pretty old. I mean like fifty, which was ancient, as it then seemed to me. He had on dirty pants and tennis shoes with knots tied in the laces. He hadn't shaved, and he was fat. His stomach stuck out. His neck was thick, but it looked puffy, not muscly. He was bald on top, but he had heavy deep sideburns, at a time when male hairstyle was running toward the sugar bowl shear.

I figured he was some kind of foreman who bossed the setting up of the show equipment. That night, when the daredevil came out of his tent to climb the tower to dive into the tank, I was astonished to see that he was the fellow I had run the errand for.

He looked different but not so much that I didn't recognize him. He had shaved and slicked his hair down on the sides. He had put on his diving costume. It was like a bodysuit, black and white. He must have had on some kind of corset because his stomach didn't stick out quite as far.

Something about him made me feel bad. I didn't want him to be an old man. A daredevil needed to be young and handsome, somebody you wanted to be like when you grew up. A daredevil certainly shouldn't be seen working like an ordinary person, tightening bolts on a tower, or driving stakes for guy wires. I wanted him to be lounging around in his hotel suite, wearing a satin robe and eating fancy food, waiting for the time to emerge and defy death.

A weak spotlight followed him up that skinny tower. At the top he stood on a little platform and looked down. He kept shifting his feet, and wiggling his arms. He waited so long to dive, we thought he had lost his nerve and might climb down. But I suppose he was only acting, letting the tension build among the spectators.

Then he did a thing that became memorable to me. He shouted a short speech and gave a plug for Cosden Gasoline, which was ablaze on the surface of the tank water. He said he needed the very best gasoline for his act, and that's why he always used Cosden. Then he dived.

The spotlight followed him down. It was a fair spectacle, but I didn't enjoy its full benefit. Because while he was in the fall, I was dealing with the realization that this daredevil operated on such a tight budget, he had to swap advertisements for enough gasoline to flame the water in his tank.

The splash seemed to douse most of the fire. He came out of that tank really quick, showing a burst of agility that encouraged me. At school the next day I felt better about him, and so I made an announcement that the daredevil was a friend of mine, and that he smoked Camels.

William's Grandmother

An interesting thing about a job like this is that it turns up old friends in unexpected places. Like in Denver, Colorado.

The way it happens, a guy who lives in Denver is in Houston on business, and when he starts home, he buys an afternoon paper at the airport. He takes it on the airplane and leaves it on the seat when he gets off.

Then this old friend of yours boards that same plane to go to Seattle to visit her daughter. She takes the seat of the gent who just rode in from Houston. She glances at the paper and sees the piece you wrote the day before.

On the way to Seattle she writes you a note, and that's how you hear from old friends you haven't seen in almost forty years.

Susan Bailey, who wore her yellow hair in braids and sat in front of me in Albert Benjamin Cunningham's creative writing class at Texas Tech. You want to know what she told me in the letter? She wrote, "I have seven grandchildren."

For crying out loud in church. Seven of them.

I have been trying to visualize what that girl looks like, now that she has become seven times a grandmother. I find it impossible to see her as a traditional granny, wearing a shawl and cloddy old shoes. Probably she wore bobby socks and saddle oxfords when I saw her last. So how can I picture her looking like Mrs. Tucker on the shortening can, or Mrs. Olsen on the TV commercials? No way.

So what I have decided is, she looks like a lady I remember as William's grandmother.

I got acquainted with William's grandmother about the same time I was sitting behind Susan Bailey in Professor Cunningham's writing class. That woman was the first contemporary grandmother I ever met. She was of immense interest to me as well as to several of my friends whose lives she touched.

My friend, William, lived with his parents there in Lubbock, and they went away for a month. William's grandmother came to stay during their absence and cook and care for William's little brothers.

To begin with, she didn't look anything like any grandmother I had ever seen. She didn't act like a grandmother, either. That woman was a perfect caution. She was great fun to know and be around.

Both my grandmothers were long gone by then, and I had loved them—but they had not been any fun to know, not for me. They wore long shapeless dresses and the customary ugly shoes and gold-rimmed spectacles that sat far down on their noses and mostly they were ladies that needed quiet. You couldn't make any noise around them.

William's grandmother was nothing like that.

She was tall and trim. She wore silk stockings and high-heeled shoes. Sometimes she wore trousers. Put on a pair of pants and go right on to the grocery store or anywhere she took a notion to go.

She used powder and paint on her face, but she knew how to do it, and she looked pretty. She didn't seem old. She dyed her hair, you could tell, but somehow that made her more interesting.

But get this: She was divorced.

A divorced grandmother. What an extraordinary idea. I thought it was wonderful. I hadn't imagined that such a thing as a divorced grandmother was in the world. The grandmothers I knew rocked in rocking chairs, and knitted, and went to church if they were well enough, and even went to picture shows that were advertised as proper. But they didn't get divorced.

And here was William's grandmother as divorced as any movie star in Hollywood. I was proud to know her.

She drove a little Chevy coupe with red wheels, and she drove it frisky, too. "Now watch this, kids," she'd say to William's little brothers. Then she'd sort of peel out in that little coupe, and the rear tires would spin a time or two and throw gravel and make a loud racket, and those boys would sure squeal. They loved it. They'd say, "Do it again, Martha."

They did that. They actually called her by her first name. None of that Grandma stuff. She wouldn't have it. "My name's Martha," she'd say, and that's what we called her. Even her grandkids seven and eight years old called her Martha.

She played tennis and golf and had been to Europe twice. Think of that, a grandmother swinging a golf club. And in Europe, at that.

You didn't have to be quiet around her. She liked noise the same as all the others of us. She could play a sort of barroom style of piano, and she would sit down there and bang those ivories and stomp her feet and grin and render an outrageous version of "Darktown Strutter's Ball," and I bet they could hear it two blocks away in the drugstore.

Knowing a noisy grandmother was sure an education.

But William was used to her and didn't class her as extraordinary at all. Sometimes he'd tell us things about her, just as a casual comment, that would snap our eyebrows. Like once he said that when she was at home, she had dates. She had a boyfriend and went out with him to picture shows and restaurants and night clubs.

Amazing. A grandmother who had dates? I'd never heard of that before and supposed there was some kind of law against it.

Of course today we have grandmothers who play golf and go dancing and ride airliners to Seattle and even run for office.

But William's grandmother was a pioneer, and I'm glad I knew her.

A Very Sad Lady

We were sitting at the long table in the neighborhood icehouse, looking out at the rain. A woman with white hair came out of the apartment building across the street. She was pretty drunk.

At least that was our guess. She might have had something else the matter with her but I doubt it. She wasn't weaving. She wasn't that drunk. She walked flat-footed, the way heavy drinkers do when they haven't gotten so drunk that they stagger. Flat-footed and real careful.

She stayed in our view about half a block. Once she stopped and appeared to show an interest in a potted plant sitting out front of an antique shop. I noticed while she was looking at the plant that she had a hand against the building, to brace herself. I don't think she was interested in the plant. I think she just needed to stop and get steady for a minute.

Mrs. T used to do that.

Mrs. T was the first woman drunkard I ever knew. She was our neighbor long ago, back in my shirttail times. Mrs. T never knew it but she taught the young people in our neighborhood a great deal about how dangerous drinking large amounts of alcohol can be. She helped us, even though she did it by being a bad example.

For a long time we thought she was sick. Her husband was dead and she lived alone in a nice white house. People said about her, "He left her well off." Meaning her husband left her comfortable in the matter of income. But she wasn't well off any other way. She stayed drunk all the time.

We would watch her come out for the paper. She wouldn't emerge to get it until almost noon. She walked the same flat-footed way as the woman on the street that I was telling you about. Slow and careful, with a stiff straight back. When she arrived at where the paper lay, she didn't simply stoop over and pick it up. She did a slow-motion descent. I watched her a lot of times. She lowered herself gradually, and then put the bracing hand out on the grass, so she wouldn't tumble over. With the other hand she would grab the paper and use it as a sort of cane, or crutch, to get herself going back up.

People who didn't know her secret would see that and say, "Poor Mrs. T, she's so sick and crippled up." Well, it was true that she was sick. But those who said that didn't understand she was an alcoholic. Not many people understood about drunks then.

Some of us who weren't but twelve or fourteen years old knew more about drunks than the Sunday school teachers who lectured us once a week about the evils of Demon Rum. Why, they didn't even know what rum was. They didn't even know what was wrong with Mrs. T.

We knew things about a drunk, thanks to Mrs. T, that

would have shocked those Sunday school teachers right out of their corsets. We knew she liked Scotch, which was hard to get in our town.

Our town was dry. We had plenty of bootleggers but they didn't deal much in Scotch. So Mrs. T would drink bourbon, or anything, when she couldn't get Scotch. One time she got onto sloe gin. Not a one of those Sunday school teachers knew what sloe gin was but we did, thanks to Mrs. T. We found out that she would even drink vanilla extract if she couldn't get any booze. We knew it because we'd find the bottles in her trash. Why would anybody throw away five or six empty vanilla extract bottles at the same time?

We knew her drinking habits because Mrs. T was always hiding bottles of booze around her premises. The reason was that sometimes her daughter came to visit and Mrs. T didn't want the daughter to find any booze in the house. So she would hide it outside.

The water meter was one of her places.

She would come out before dark to put bottles in the hole where the water meter was. She seemed to think it had already gotten dark. Sometimes we would know more about what was in the water meter than she did. Because she would forget. I used to impress my friends by taking them to Mrs. T's water meter at night and showing them what she had stashed in there. Maybe two or three pints.

Sometimes, and this was pitiful, she would think she had hidden a bottle when it wasn't hidden at all. Like she'd put it behind a post on the back porch when she was drunk, and I suppose she thought she had concealed it. When in fact it would be sitting there glinting in the sun by ten o'clock the next morning.

Mrs. T gave me an early experience in bootlegging. I didn't know I was having anything to do with bootlegging until I had already done it. She called me to her back door and said I could make fifty cents if I would go to the north part of town on my bicycle and bring her a package.

In those times, I would have gone anywhere on my bicycle for fifty cents. We had grown men, with families, working for two bucks a day. But Mrs. T did not know much about prices so I got half a dollar for delivering a sloshy package to her from the bootlegger's house back behind the depot.

From watching that poor lady, we learned that drunks are not the way we thought they were. We thought they always came staggering and weaving along the street, laughing and talking loud and having a good time, until finally they fell in the gutter and passed out.

Mrs. T never staggered. She certainly never talked loud, or laughed. She was a very sad lady.

Mr. Weatherford's Secret

The last few days, I suppose because of this go-fishing kind of weather we've been having, I've thought a good deal about Mr. Weatherford. He was a good-natured gent who lived in our old hometown back when my gang was in overalls and tennis shoes. Mr. Weatherford loved fishing.

Among the parents of our town, he was known for being "good about" things. Your mother would say, "Mr. Weatherford is good about taking the boys fishing." Or "Mr. Weatherford is good about paying attention to the children."

It's true he took a lot of us fishing. At this season he would go to the river two or three times a month and he would always take along at least a couple of boys out of my bunch. I went half a dozen trips, I guess. We would go mostly to the Brazos, up in Palo Pinto County close to where Possum Kingdom Lake is now. Sometimes we'd go to the Colorado, between Brownwood and Brady. We'd go and camp out and spend two or three nights.

Mr. Weatherford had this old Model A truck. He'd come around to our houses and collect the various boys he'd agreed to take along. He would always talk to the parents and tell them not to worry, these boys'll be all right. And your mother would say, "Now you behave, and do what Mr. Weatherford says, you hear?" Yes ma'am.

When we got to the river, he would make his little speech. I heard it several times, same speech. It was made through or around a wad of Beechnut chewing tobacco. And it was punctuated with expectoration. Later on, after I failed to get honest work and took up writing instead, I would try to record Mr. Weatherford's speeches on paper. I discovered his sentences had no commas. In place of commas they had spits. Patoo. That was his comma.

"Now boys (patoo) somethin' you boys got to find out about comin' to the river like this to have a good time (patoo) you got to do a little work first. So let's us get unloaded and set camp up and gather our firewood and seine us some bait and after that (patoo) we'll wet us a few hooks."

So we'd fall to and unload. He had an old green wooden boat on the truck. It wasn't but about twelve feet long but that vessel must have weighed what a new bass boat does now. We'd unload the tackle and the bedrolls and the grub box and all the other gear and it was mucho manual labor.

When I say "we," that pronoun does not include Mr. Weatherford. I am unable to see him lifting as much as a bait bucket. While we did the work, he found a stump to sit on. He would sit there digging with thumb and forefinger into his package of Beechnut, issuing orders and spitting commas.

"Now boys (patoo) easy with that coal oil lantern. You break that light and we won't have anything to see by but our fire. Now then (patoo) let's gather us up a bed of those leaves and we'll use 'em for a mattress. If you boys been to church lately (patoo) I hope you didn't pray for no rain. It sure does look wet in the northeast."

He had a kind face but I didn't like to look at it much because of the tobacco. Two deep creases curved down his chin from the corners of his mouth and often they were channels carrying his Beechnut juice. When I would glance at him I always saw somebody taking a warm wet rag and wiping the tobacco out of his creases, the way your mother would wash around your mouth when you were a very small child.

I think now, knowing more about how bodies feel when they age, I think Mr. Weatherford hurt a lot. He was overweight and couldn't bend. And I know his feet bothered him. I see him getting out of that truck, ever so careful and slow, as if he wondered whether his legs would support him when finally he arrived on the ground. He wore khakis and a greasy old cow-working hat and black hightop shoes, with white socks.

He'd sit on his stump and direct us when we seined bait. "Now what you want is them red horse minners (patoo) bigger the better. Swing out wide with that far stick. Keep 'er down. Keep 'at stick on the bottom. You worried about water mocksins (patoo) they can't bite you underwater."

Which was bad information but he didn't know it.

The only work he did, he'd get in the boat and oversee the baiting of the trotlines. He'd hold a paddle, mostly for steering. He'd see that we didn't do anything dumb (patoo) and get hooked by the trotline.

Through his Beechnut he talked to us about roundups, stampedes, panthers, rattlesnakes. He showed us how to skin a catfish. How to cook a potato in the coals of the fire. How to put an elm stick over the coffee pot to keep it from boiling over.

You see why (patoo) don't you? Why he took us? It was the only way he could go. He couldn't do the labor of going alone. I think very likely he'd rather have been on the river with men his own age, with his old friends. But he couldn't bear to have them do his part of the work. So he took us.

In my judgment, now, it was a bargain for those of us he took. He was bad about giving orders and being waited on. He would have us get up and bring him his fresh socks out of the truck. But he was patient. He never criticized us so that it hurt. He was good about that.

He Drew a Check

According to what I read in the paper, pretty soon we will all be paying our bills through some kind of computerized system, instead of sending checks in the mail. So we're moving toward a day when we won't be writing checks any longer. I will not grieve when that day arrives. Bank checks have always given me trouble.

The trouble began with the first check I ever touched. This was in 1935. One of our milk cows was threatening to have a calf and my parents promised that the calf would be mine. I had never owned anything before.

I was not pleased by the lecture that went along with the promise. They said if the calf was a heifer it could be the start of my own herd of dairy cattle. If it was a bull I could sell it and buy something of value, such as a pair of shoes.

We were going to church a lot then. When everybody else was praying and giving thanks for blessings and ask-

ing forgiveness for sins, I was asking God to make the calf
a bull. Because I sure didn't want to start any herds of dairy
cattle. Dairy cows had to be milked twice a day, seven days
a week, and always at uncivilized hours. I'd already had
my fill of that.

It turned out that God was good and made the calf a
bull and I sold it to a fellow in striped overalls and a straw
hat. He gave me a check for three dollars. I watched him
write it. He *drew* it more than wrote it. He used a short
cedar pencil he carried in a curious way, jammed between
the top of his ear and the side of his head.

I took the check to Mr. Hill at the bank and he said it
was no good. He explained that sometimes people wrote
checks when they didn't have any money in the bank and
that was how a check could be bad.

He said I had some choices on what to do. I could take
the check back to the fellow who wrote it and see if he
would give me cash instead. Or I could try to get my calf
back. Or I could wait and see if the fellow put any money
in the bank to make the check good.

I didn't go to see that man. I was about half afraid to.
And I sure didn't want the calf back. We already had more
livestock than I was interested in fooling with. I wanted to
play ball, not milk cows.

So every day or two I would return to the bank and try
to cash the check. It would not cash. I took it back so often
that all I had to do was step inside the door and Mr. Hill
would see me and shake his head.

The check kept getting dimmer and dirtier and finally
it tore in half where I folded and unfolded it so often. I
mended it with paste.

When my father came home—he was forever gone on
long trips in his traveling salesman's job—I told him about
the check and he was silent a while. Then he said, "We'll
see about that."

The next morning we drove out to the place where the

fellow in the striped overalls lived. My father took what was left of the check and went in that house. After just a short time he came out and handed me three limp dollar bills.

We went straight to town and spent them, for some school pants and a pair of tennis shoes. I remember what the tennis shoes cost—$1.29. So the pants had to cost less than $2.00.

Among people of my generation that kind of experience created in us a sort of Depression intellect. Even now when a guy gives me a personal check I can't help wondering if it's any good.

◆───────────────────────────◆

Why Were They Angry?

Back when Herbert Hoover was president and Model-T Fords were still cadillacking around the courthouse square on Saturday afternoons, we lived near a big family by the name of Jordan. They pronounced it JERD-un.

We talked about the Jordans a lot in our house because something interesting was always going on over there. They were forever laughing or fussing or yelling or building something or tearing something down.

Sometimes fights would break out among the childrn, and these were worth your while to watch. Generally they would start indoors and be continued in the yard because Mrs. Jordan had a rule about fighting in the house.

I can hear her now, stating the rule to a couple of her kids, "If you're gonna fight, go outside." She hardly raised her voice, saying that. She always sounded tired to me, and I expect she was.

What got me thinking about the Jordans, on a recent Sunday afternoon I was driving near the little Austin

County town of Industry and came across a big family soft-ball game, being played in a pasture. Must have been twenty folks on each side. There were grandmothers and grandfathers in the outfield and little girls not seven years old playing shortstop and pretty young mamas at bat. Everybody in the family was in that game, and it was a good thing to see. I wanted to stop and find out what the score was.

The Jordans used to have big family ball games that way. Sometimes on weekends there would be Jordans by the dozen come in for a gathering, and after Sunday dinner they would choose up and have this noisy ball game in the yard for hours. The game was played then with what we called an indoor ball. It was larger than a standard softball and had raised rawhide seams that could peel back a fin-gernail if you didn't watch out. Nobody used a glove, even though that ball when new was hard as any baseball used today in the big leagues.

The Jordans at play made a colorful scene. They played in whatever they wore to church that morning. The men took off their coats and loosened their ties and ran around the bases in their patent leather shoes and black trousers and white shirts. The women played in nice dresses, but some would take off their shoes and go barefoot.

I used to sit in our backyard and watch those games and yearn to go over and slip into left field and try to catch a fly. But nobody walked up uninvited and got into a Jor-dan family game. You just knew not to do it. This was a closed enterprise, and nobody allowed but Jordans.

A couple of those boys were about my age, and they were good athletes, not big but quick and feisty, with fire in their eyes and short-fused tempers. All the Jordans were that way. The word among boys at school was that you better not mess with the Jordans if you didn't enjoy a fistfight.

Oh, they were friendly enough in calm times. But when you paid close attention you could detect a quiet seething, just beneath their surface, and you knew it wouldn't take much of a spark to detonate all that anger.

I liked hanging around with the Jordans, though, because they were so different from my own family and that was a fascination. We didn't have much anger in our house, and when we did have a little we smothered it in painful silence. My folks not only didn't allow fighting in the house, they didn't allow it outside, either. So the Jordans were an education for me.

Before I knew them, the physical fighting I had done and watched was school playground stuff, consisting mostly of pushing and shoving and grunting and rolling in the dirt. But the Jordans were punchers, headhunters. They didn't go charging in on an opponent, with arms flailing like most boys did. They jabbed you. They reminded me of snakes striking, the way those skinny arms and sharp elbows would shoot out and deliver a stinging pop on a guy's jaw and draw back in a flicker. All the Jordan boys seemed to know how to do that from the time they could throw a punch.

They played ball that same quick way. They didn't mind choking up on the bat to get a compact swing and punch hot little liners out over second base. And run? Lordy they could run. No, not like deer. Like rabbits. They scurried. Start and stop and turn so quick they'd take an extra base on you if you reached up to rub your eye.

Not many young boys wanted to play like that. They all wanted to hold the bat down at the end and swing big and try to hit homers, and I expect they're still that way.

So the Jordans to me were extraordinary people, and I learned a good deal from them. What I never did find out about them was why they were so angry.

A Sweet Shattery Noise

On my car radio I often get commercials read by Pat Sum-merall, the former football star. He raised my eyebrows a few degrees the other afternoon by speaking the following sentence into a microphone: "Nobody likes to hear the sound of breaking glass."

That surprised me because any citizen who has been around as long as Pat Summerall has got to know that breaking glass makes a sound that's dear to many ears, especially to the ears of young boys.

Back in my early times, out on the T&P Railroad west of Fort Worth, the sound of breaking glass was ranked as a highly satisfactory noise. At least it was by the gang of dudes that I ran with. We'd as soon chunk a rock and bust a bottle as swing a bat and crack a two-base hit.

In those sweet times out there in that Cross Timbers Country, we had a lot of abandoned farm houses with sagging roofs and crumbling chimneys and nobody cared anything about them. I suppose there was a trespass law then but we didn't know about it and nobody ever came around to enforce it. Sometimes bums off the railroad would stay in those old places but mostly they were empty and some of them had window panes that made an excellent racket when you hit one with a rock.

Naturally I am not recommending that anybody go around chunking windows out of old houses. You would get arrested for it, because an old house in the country now is classed a wonderful thing to own and to spend money on and you mustn't break its windows out.

But these were rickety old houses that nobody valued. You could set a match to one and burn it to ashes and not a fire department in the county would waste a quart of water on it. Although I am here to say I never set a match to any house. I am just talking about the difference in the way people looked at old houses, then and now.

A young guy in our bunch could earn respect by being able to knock out a window pane with a rock. Today he must throw passes or fast balls. But in this time I am talking about, he could chunk rocks and create the sound of breaking glass and be a hero among his peers.

But you understand there was sportsmanship involved. You had to back off a considerable distance before you chunked, if you wanted any recognition. A guy who got up close enough to poke out a window with a stick was asking to be disqualified and disgraced.

Even on our schoolyard there was a measure of distinction a guy could earn by breaking a window pane. But he had to do it in an honorable way and I will tell you how it was done.

Our school took a long lunch hour. This was because most of the students went home to eat, and some to do chores. For example, I had to go get the milk cow from the vacant lot where I had staked her before I went to school. I took her in and watered her and took her back out to another vacant lot that had plenty of Johnson grass. Then I'd grab something to eat and run back to school. Run, sure, but not because I was eager to return to class. I wanted to be there in time to get in on the ball game before the bell rang.

We had this wonderful game of scrub baseball every day at noon. Anybody who wanted to could play. We called it scrub but I now hear it called workup. Might be forty-five players. I loved this game with a fierceness. Running back to school, I would feel that if I didn't get there in time to have a try at a fly ball, I would just die from disappointment.

The goal of this noon-hour game was to work up to bat and knock the ball so far into left field that it hit and broke a window in the high school auditorim.

When anybody did it, he had to pay for the window. Even so, he swung mightily to do it, and got an ovation if he did.

I never did, I hate to say. But it was an important goal for me. Sometimes I would dream about doing it. Almost the entire student body would be watching and I would drive one deep, deep, and it would hit an auditorium window pane just exactly right and the sound of the glass breaking would be exquisite because it would mean I was a noon-hour hero.

The guy who broke a window that way would stay a hero for two or three hours, which was way longer that I had ever been one. He would also be obliged to report to the principal's office and confess (with pride, but it wasn't supposed to show) that he had knocked a window out.

I have been trying to establish, on the telephone, what one of those small window panes cost. I believe it was on the order of seventy-five cents. I certainly couldn't have shucked six bits out of my pants pocket but I would have been proud to owe the school system that amount. Probably it would be written on the record, and I couldn't ever have paid it. So then the archives would show, even yet, that in 1938 I hit one hard enough to break a window pane in left field.

Nobody playing now in the major leagues would be prouder of a home run than I would have been if I could have broken one of those windows, and heard the sweet shattering of glass.

Bums for Dinner

Back in the thirties there were railroad bums who would come to our house for Christmas dinner. They were quiet men with good manners.

My mother was running a boardinghouse then and cooked three meals a day, seven days a week, fifty-two weeks a year. Most of the boarders were also roomers and slept upstairs in the big frame steamboat of a house where we were living.

The female roomers and boarders were schoolteachers and they would leave town when school turned out a few days before Christmas. The male ones worked at the power plant, which never shut down, so we'd always have one or two of them in town for Christmas.

So in those boardinghouse times, during the holidays the table in that old house had fewer diners than on ordinary workdays. A lot of food would be left over from Christmas dinner and the railroad bums were fed out of this surplus. They didn't come in and eat at the table. They ate on the back steps.

I knew where they stayed when they were in town. The place was in a heavy thicket of briars and shin oak down by the T&P depot. We always heard that you could go down there in the hobo jungle and turn over boards and find the addresses of houses where a bum could knock on the back door and get a free meal. I never found any such thing written on a board, though, and I turned over a good many of them, hoping to find our own address. If anybody's address was advertised that way it ought to have been ours because my mother fed an army of these sad guys. I didn't understand the main reason she did it until after she died.

I used to find something to do in the backyard when these fellows were eating on our steps. So I could watch them. They were dressed in a curious style, in pants and coats that didn't match or fit very well. It was common to see a man with two shirts on, or even three if you looked close. I suppose three old shirts felt good if you didn't have a winter coat.

Stories I'd read about railroad bums said they had great tales to tell about the places they'd been and the things they'd seen. But the men who ate on our back steps didn't tell stories. They ate in silence. They ate in a methodical way, as if eating was just one of the processes of staying alive, like breathing, and the taste of the food didn't matter.

They ate all of what was put on their plates. Their system was to save for last a piece of bread and wipe up every trace of gravy or dressing or cranberry sauce. When a hobo finished eating, his plate didn't appear to need washing. It looked like a big dog had licked it clean.

Then he would put down the plate and the knife and the fork and regard them with what I thought was reverence, for several seconds. I don't know, maybe it wasn't reverence. Maybe he was just looking to make sure he hadn't missed anything. Or guessing how long it would be before he saw another plate full of food.

The only one of those hobos I remember by name is Mr. Martin. That might have been a first name instead of a last. It's the only one he ever gave. I remember him because he stayed around three or four days one Christmas and fixed the fence on our cow lot to pay for his meals. At night he would go back down by the railroad tracks to sleep but by the time we got up to milk the next morning, he would be out there working on the fence.

I hung around him a lot, thinking he might tell me stories about his adventures on the road. But all he ever talked about to me was his "place." He'd say, "Now when I had my place . . . " Meaning a home, I guess, and a family.

My mother surprised me at Christmas by asking Mr. Martin to come into the dining room and eat with us. He refused, and stayed on the back steps.

Years afterward, when both my parents had died, I asked one of my older sisters if she remembered the Christmas our mother invited that hobo into our house, and she did remember. She thought the reason was that Mr. Martin reminded our mother of one of her brothers who had gone wandering years before and was never heard from.

"Every time she fed a hobo," my sister said, "I think she was praying that somebody was doing the same for her brother."

◆————————————————————————◆

My Friend Munroe

We were the same age, about twelve, when Munroe began coming to our neighborhood several times a week. He came with his mother, who washed and ironed and cleaned house and cooked. Not in my family's house. In another house down the street.

What drew him to our yard was the football. I'd gotten a football for Christmas and he'd wander up and sit at the end of the hedge and watch us play. I wonder now if he'd ever touched a football before then. I doubt it.

But from the first time that ball bounced his way, he could kick and pass and catch it better than any of the others of us. A natural athlete. Tall for his age, maybe a couple of inches taller than I was then, and he had those long

muscles that so many good athletes have. I spent two summers trying to do something better, in the matter of sports,
than Munroe could. I never did.

This was 1934 and 1935, in West Texas, so all those
bizarre rules of racial separation were a part of our social
structure. But the rules applied to minors in a strange fashion. They were more complex than the rules governing
adults.

For example: Two thirteen-year-old boys, one white
and one black, kicking a football in the street wouldn't
draw any special notice in our town. But the place where
the football was being kicked was significant. The street,
that was okay. If they happened to be playing in somebody's yard, that was a little different. It might cause the
head of a passerby to turn, see who those boys were, playing together in the yard that way. If the boys went to the
playground of the white school to kick the ball, even on
a Saturday, that was getting close to a violation. And for
a black youngster to play on the white schoolyard when
school was going on—well, it just wasn't done.

Munroe and I never talked about the rules but we
knew them.

That first winter I had the football, we came close to
wearing the thing out in the street. We played a two-man
kicking game popular then. You tried to back your opponent to his goal by outkicking him, and then to score you
had to drop-kick over the line.

Drop-kicking is almost never seen now but a good
dropkicker was held in high regard in the time of Munroe
and me. I bet Munroe was the best teen-aged dropkicker
in creation. My guess is, though, he never got to play in
an organized football game. Too bad.

Munroe did not go into our house, ever. When I
would go in for a minute he would say that he'd wait
outside.

From Munroe I began to learn a bit, just a suggestion, of what it meant to be black in our town. One day I went with him to the house where his mother was working. We went to the back door. His mother was cooking fried pies. She gave us one and told us to sit on the back steps and eat it and we did.

I knew the family that lived in that house. If I had come to the house alone I would have gone to the front door. If they had given me a fried pie I would have eaten it at the table where the family ate. But since I came with Munroe I went to the back door and sat outside and ate the pie.

I would prefer to remember that I was outraged by this discrimination. But I really wasn't. I mainly felt that it was interesting, to share with Munroe that small black experience. It seemed to me a curious privilege I had as a white—that I could go with Munroe and feel black for a couple of minutes, but he could not go with me and feel white.

Two or three times Munroe took me to his house. It always smelled like turnips cooking. I mentioned that and Munroe said they had been eating lots and lots of turnips lately.

One time I went to a black softball game that Munroe played in. My father took me. My father liked going to black affairs because they always seated him on the front row and made him feel special. I was not comfortable on the front row. When Munroe came to white softball games he sat down the first-base line, away from the white folks. When we came to black games, we sat on the front row behind the plate. But I didn't say anything to my father because he liked the system.

The only time I got as angry as I should have gotten was when I visited Munroe's school. It was really bad. It was disgraceful. Even so, I didn't imagine there was anything I could ever do about it. And I was angry only for Munroe, not for the other black kids.

So my awareness of racial injustice was that limited. But it was a beginning, and Munroe was the reason for it.

III

A PLACE IN THE WOODS

Testing, Testing

Hello from the front porch of an old house in the country. It's ten o'clock in the morning. Temperature is 64. Southeast wind variable at 5 to 10 m.p.h. To ask for a nicer day in the middle of January would be greedy.

I'm here to test myself. I've been testing for two weeks, trying to find out if I'd like to live in the country. For years I've been close to buying a little plot of woods, but before I could get a down payment made, I would cool off on the idea.

So I decided to make this test. I leased a country house for six months. I intend to stay here for as much of the lease period as my duties will allow, and see if I end up loving it or hating it. Half a year ought to make a pretty good trial.

So far, I can say the test has been part fun and part lonesome. But it's all been interesting.

The village of Winedale is a mile and a quarter from where I sit. It's the nearest community that shows on my road map.

Winedale is in Fayette County and I am just across the line in the southwest part of Washington County. So I am associated here with various towns. With Brenham, because it's the county seat of Washington. With Industry in Austin County, because I pay my phone bill to the Industry Telephone Company. With Giddings, because I pay my light bill to the Bluebonnet Electric Co-op there.

If I had a rural mail box, which I don't, my address would be Route 2, Burton. If I had a minor dependent here, which I don't have either, she or he would go to school at Carmine. To buy stamps, I go to the post office at Round Top. Also I can buy a *Chronicle* there, at Klump's Grocery.

When my cooking gets dreary, I go to Wagner's Store in Winedale. I do not know a hamburger anywhere in the state that beats the burgers that Marilyn Wagner cooks. Yesterday I had two meals. For lunch I had a Marilyn Wagner hamburger and for supper I had another one.

You might like this house, if you love old houses.

My landlord is George Dillingham of Brenham. A few years ago he and his wife Cassie fixed this house up as a weekend place. It sits on thirteen woody acres. Originally it was a two-room frontier house. A third room has been tacked on to make a modern kitchen. So the house has three rooms in a row, and the oldest part goes back to about 1850.

That I don't really care about. Two things about this place I like. One is the front porch, which is 54 feet

3 inches long. The other thing is the little creek behind the house. It meanders in outrageous S-curves through heavy growths of post oak, cedar, yaupon, live oak, and black-jack. Coons live along there, and opossums, and twenty dozen sorts of birds. Deer pass through, and coyotes.

My first night, several coyotes put their muzzles to-gether within fifty yards of the kitchen and offered me a twenty-second rendition of their goblin music. I appreci-ated that welcome but I can't listen to those sounds with-out getting tingles up the sides of my neck.

Sometimes I've had visitors from Houston but I've spent a lot of these two weeks alone, getting acquainted with this house. I wasn't sure it liked me, at first. A person alone in an eccentric house needs time to learn it and get comfortable with it. At night, especially.

I needed to understand, when I was in the kitchen washing dishes after supper, that nobody was really rap-ping on the window pane in the bedroom at the other end of the house. It was the wind, popping the glass in the windows. They are old and have lost their putty and like to rattle in their frames.

Then at night, lying half-awake in the west end, I heard two—no, three—stealthy footsteps on the porch at the east end. I got out of bed, reached for the flashlight. Went to challenge the intruder.

No intruder was there. The stealthy footsteps were produced by a limb of the live oak at the southeast corner of the porch. The wind was making it thump on the roof.

Being isolated stirs the imagination. I am very likely staying in one of the safest places on the continent. But be-fore I moved in, I talked on the phone to old friend Belton Hightower. He has lived alone several years in the country between Brenham and Somerville. I asked him what kind of weapon I ought to get, since I was going to stay out here in the woods by myself.

He said: "I've got a gun you can use. I haven't shot anybody with it in a good while. I've just about quit shootin' people."

Which was his way of telling me I don't need a gun. So I don't have one. I have a lot of other very effective weapons, though, that I will tell you about when I get enough space.

Here comes my neighbor to the north, Herb Gilley, to bring me some dry cedar to burn in my stove. He has been here twice now, to see if I'm all right. If I decide I don't like living in the country it won't be on account of the people, who have been mighty neighborly.

Well, I have got to wind this up and go split some kindling. See you at the post office.

Sounds, Dogs, Etc.

Sunday morning, and I'm sitting on the front porch again at the old house in the country. The wind is out of the south and carrying the smell of spring.

The clouds are traveling lower and lower. I think they'll bring a shower. I hope so, because the roof on this old house is metal and I like to hear the rain on it. I heard sleet on it when I stayed here two weeks back in January. Made an interesting tink-tink-tink sound. I have got my little recorder handy, hoping to capture the racket of a hailstorm if I ever get one.

I'm going into my third month now of living in the country, as a half-year test to see if I might want to move out of Houston and live permanently in a place like this. I have to say it hasn't yet been much of a test because about the time I come up here and get settled, something happens that sends me hurrying back to town.

Last time it was this little computer that I work on. I did something that offended it and it spit up all its programs, including the one that enables me to send this stuff to the *Chronicle* on the telephone. So I had to pack up and go back and get it programmed again. Computers are wonderful to work on but you've got to be nice to them or they'll turn on you.

I feel healthier here than I do in Houston and I suppose it's because I get so much sleep. I haven't found a lot to do at night except go to bed and read until the book falls and hits me in the stomach. Then I turn off the light. I don't have a television here and I won't get one because I'm afraid I'd start watching it during the day when I'm supposed to be working.

So when the first cardinal gives his wake-up call just before dawn, I am usually already conscious. Peterson's *Birds of Texas* suggests that the cardinal is saying, "What CHEER, what CHEER, what CHEER." I'll accept that. Cardinals make a lot of other comments, though.

I like to be out here on the porch early, when the bluebirds fly over. They're always way high, sending down their soft gurgles. Beautiful but sad notes. Peterson wants me to hear them saying, "Purity, purity, purity." Sometimes I can hear that but most times bluebirds say to me, "Choy-yoy, choy-yoy." I hope that's not an obscenity in Chinese.

When I was here in January and the weather was cold, I had a big handful of beef tallow that I'd trimmed off about four pounds of stew meat. The bird folks are always saying tallow is good for birds in cold weather so I put that stuff out. I put it on the tops of posts in the yard fence behind the kitchen and forgot about it.

Next morning I happened to remember my tallow and looked out to see what kind of pretty songbirds were enjoying my charity. Surely the cardinals, which provide me with such pleasant wake-up calls. Maybe one of those

sweet-voiced bluebirds. Might even be a tanager or a gold-
finch, or one of the buntings with all those blue and red
and green feathers.

What I had were four buzzards.

They were sitting, hump-shouldered, all in a row on
top of my fence posts, waiting to see if the posts were going to sprout any more tallow. I have put out tallow twice
since then and didn't feed anything but vultures, so I
have quit.

In the middle of the preceding paragraph I heard what
sounded like a jet airplane, flying low, coming this way.
Turned out to be only a surge of wind stirring the cedars
on the other side of the road.

Gradually I am learning the sounds of this place. On
a weekday morning when a roar approaches from the
southeast and the front porch trembles, I know that's the
school bus coming. It's a small bus but it somehow makes
everything shiver when it sails by on the gravel road at a
sharp clip.

I am also learning to distinguish vehicles that pass by
my front gate. Early this morning I saw Harry Ullrich, my
neighbor to the south, going by in his old Chevy. On his
way to Round Top to buy a newspaper.

One of the ways I know it was Mr. Ullrich, as soon as
the Chevy goes by his yellow dog comes off the hill and
wags up to my porch to visit. This dog and I are already
pretty fair friends.

One of the dog's eyes is brown, and the other is a
milky blueish-white, what dog people call a glass eye.
That glass-eye characteristic is being passed around among
country dogs now. The first of these glass eyes I ever saw
were on leopard cowdogs I watched in the fifties. They
were working wild cattle in the Navasota River bottom.
One glass eye on a yellow dog, like this one sleeping here

now on my porch, gives the animal a really extraordinary appearance.

I've been trying the best I can to be a good country citizen, but the first thing I've done is let my light bill get overdue. As a customer of Bluebonnet Electric Co-op, I'm supposed to read my own meter and send in the money to Giddings before the fifteenth of the month. I couldn't get back up here in time to do it. A black mark against my credit already.

I'm sorry about that because I like doing business with an outfit that takes my word for how much power I've used.

This Is a Cold House

The last deadline of 1986 has caught me in the old farmhouse where I've sat on the front porch a good many mornings during the past year and watched the sun come up. I'm not on the porch this morning. Little too chilly.

Sitting in the kitchen instead, close to the cookstove, with my chair backed up to the oven. It's now seven o'clock on New Year's Eve morning.

I'd rather be by the wood stove in the middle room because I can hear the fire popping and talking and wanting me to come be with it. But I've got guests in there still sleeping. We're going to welcome the new year here in the country, with a banquet of chili, pinto beans, and yellow corn bread, plus black-eyed peas for dessert.

I'm feeling a little smart-alec right now because I passed one of the hardest tests that a host in an old country house is ever given: Building a wood fire in an iron stove early on a cold morning without waking guests asleep in the same room. That ain't easy, Mildred. There is no way to touch an iron stove with a poker or a stick of wood that it won't respond with a ringing clank that sends waves of racket to both ends of the house.

Something I've enjoyed about having this old house is, it's been educational to city friends.

Do you know that we have native Texans forty years old or more who don't know how it feels to get up early in the morning in a cold house? It's true. They were born into air conditioning and central heat and have never been out of it. I was astonished to learn we have people like that living in Houston. It's good for them to spend a night in a leaky old shell of a house, and feel the cold nipping their toes when they get up to go to the bathroom.

I invite them up here, a captive audience, and lecture them about how things were in the country when I was young. There is nothing they can do but listen, and say, "My, my" and "You don't mean it."

One of my best stories is about the glass of water on the window sill. That was the night I woke up thirsty at 2:00 a.m. and reached for the water I'd left by the bed and it had frozen solid, right there in the house. And that didn't happen in the frigid North. It happened in Central Texas.

In those times, it did not occur to people to keep a house warm during the night. A purebred blizzard could be going on, but at bedtime the fires were banked, the stoves were shut down, and the house sent into refrigeration.

Sometimes I tell the one about the toilet popping off the wall. This really gets them. Even the children will listen to this one.

That happened in the early years of indoor plumbing. The privy had been torn down and chopped up and burned for kindling in the fireplace. One corner of a bed-room was partitioned off for a bathroom, and a commode and tub were installed.

Then here came a double-jointed, four-engine blizzard and wrecked the new bathroom. Water in the commode froze, and the tank shattered, and the toilet bowl cracked like the shell of an egg and divided itself into four equal parts, and everybody gathered to see the damage and talk about the privy and how they wished it hadn't been burned, and that was a winter that lived in infamy, the time the toilet froze.

On the coldest nights here in the country I give lessons in the Uncle Barney Hale method of getting up in the morning. My Uncle Barney taught me this when I was about ten and he was staying at our house. It's his method of getting dressed without exposing any bare hide to the cold.

He kept all his clothes on a chair by the bed and slept in long-john underwear. When he woke up, first thing he did was reach out and get his hat and put it on. Next he'd get his socks and pull those on, beneath the covers. Then he'd sit up and put on his shirt. Next he drew the covers up from the foot of the bed and brought his pants into play from below and yanked 'em on, and he was then in a position to swing his feet off the bed and directly into his shoes without ever touching the cold floor.

Well, I see my guests are awake, and so I must renew the coffee pot and put on the beans and get ready for the celebration.

What Would Papa Think?

This old house is full of cracks and mouse holes and it needs a few more storm windows before I'd care to do much wintering in it.

We've got storm windows on the north side now and they've made a lot of difference. In January of '85, when I was staying up here full time, trying to get a book done, the north wind would come through those windows as if they were wide open, and make the curtains stand out like flags in a hurricane. Didn't take me long to enjoy as much of that as I could stand.

The new windows will get another test tonight. As we used to say, sitting on other front porches of old houses similar to this, it's afixin' to git cold. The darkness in the sky to the northwest is looking like a blue whistler.

I've been sitting here wondering what my dead father would think about me, paying out money to rent an ancient country house like this when I already have a comfortable place to live in town. He was born in such a house, and at the age of twelve was already struggling to get away from that old place, and from hard times and the countriness it represented.

He would have loved living in Houston. The great buildings and the freeways and the lights at Christmas would have been a wonder to him. You think the traffic would have bothered him? No way. He'd have counted it a marvel, all those shiny cars going round and round, never having flats or blowouts or vapor locks.

And here I am straining my budget to rent the kind of place he worked so hard to escape from. Place that doesn't

even have a television set. I doubt he could have understood that. Doing without TV, I mean, by choice.

I remember when they got the television set, only four
months before my mother died. Now hear this: She felt
that one of the great blessings of her life was seeing Billy
Graham preach on TV.

For four more years, that TV glowed and flickered and
vertical-rolled at the foot of my father's bed. It was his companion. He was in love with it. I can forgive television for
all its sins because of what it does for old people. It may be
ruining our children but it comforts the spirits of the eld-
erly who are ill and can't go out and about.

I'm not sure I could explain to my father why I like to
come here and sit on this porch and do without what he
counted to be miracles of technology. It has something to
do, partly, with him. When I'm here alone I feel close to
him because, I suppose, this is the sort of environment in
which he began.

Beyond that, coming here satisfies my hankering to be
closer to natural wonders. I can see and feel the rhythm of
the land better here than I can in the city. The coming and
going of the foliage on the post oaks and elms. The sprouting and the maturing of native grasses. The arrival and departure of migratory birds.

The last three weeks these woods have been working
alive with robins. Hundreds of them, chirping in the trees.
These birds are an entertainment. I hear them right now.

Robins care about each other. They want to be together. A robin is forever on the watch for another robin.
Two can meet at an altitude of 150 feet, going opposite directions, and they both try to turn around and go the way
the other is headed. They need to be together.

I can't recall my parents, or any of my forepeople,
speaking of such things. Probably they were so close to

nature they considered its processes to be ordinary and dependable and permanent.

But I have become enthusiastic about the normal course of nature. Maybe this is because the normal course is threatened by the very technology that my father admired.

You want to know what I've seen this trip that made me feel the best? Tiny green leaves, looking healthy and good, hunkered down in poor-soiled places. At this time of year they keep low to the ground for protection. You know what they are? Bluebonnet plants, sprouting before Christmas so we'll have blooms in April.

A Change of Heart

Less than a month ago I drove up here to this old country house that I've been paying rent on now for almost two years and I came near turning around and going back to Houston before I unloaded.

I sat on the front porch, where I'm sitting right now, and had a fuss with myself about why I keep paying out hard money for this place. Temperature was sitting on about 94. Sky was a washed-out gray. The live oaks had a coating of dust on their leaves. The yard was seared. Grasshoppers were deserting the territory. They'd already destroyed what was left of the garden.

"What's so great about this place?" I asked myself. Myself replied, "Not much. It's not any better than being in Houston."

It sure wasn't. Everything around me was tired and thirsty. A jaybird came and sat on a fence post. His beak was hanging open and I thought I could see his tongue hanging out. Even the dirt daubers and the yellow jackets had quit working.

I walked down to the creek and it was all dried up except for a few sad little pools. The dog was with me and she jumped into one of the pools and came up looking surprised, and covered with some kind of gray-green scummy stuff, and I had to wash her off. I was paying rent for this kind of fun?

That night I couldn't sleep for the heat. Electric fan would keep me cool on top but I'd wake up lying in a puddle of sweat. Before dawn I surrendered and got up. Stuck one leg into my jeans that had spent the night hanging on a chair and instantly I felt sharp little pains all along my hide, from my foot to way up on my thigh.

Fire ants. Scores of the little boogers had come up through a hole in the floor and invaded my jeans. Thought I'd never get those dang-busted, gad-blasted, clod-pitchin' ants off my carcass. Stung me about twenty times. Looked like I had smallpox on one leg.

So I loaded up and went back to Houston. At least in Houston I could sleep without flesh-eating creatures invading my clothes. On the way back I added up all the rent I've paid on the place the last two years, and the total made me feel bad. Rent's way too high anyway. Who needs to pay that much to get stung by twenty fire ants before breakfast?

I didn't come back up here for about a month. Took that long before the fire ant stings quit itching. But in that time, things happened. Rains came, first. Washed off the live oaks and the grass and weeds. Scoured the creek and got rid of the scum. Seven kinds of grass revived and put up fall foilage and seed heads. New wildflowers appeared—flowers that prefer the fall over the spring.

What's happened to this old place is October. Which is often a magic month in this state.

The radio tells me there's snow in New England right now, and here in Washington County we are benefiting from the leading edge of the cold air mass that has brought winter to the Yankees. We have got one of those sweet early cold fronts that makes our world a different and truly livable place.

Sitting here on the front porch, I must remind myself that I didn't like this house a month ago. I love it now.

The sky that was so depressing in early September? It's been transformed into a pure, cool blue. The only clouds in it are condensation trails from the jets that streak across, six miles high.

The norther has improved my sight. Distant objects are clearly drawn. Trees. Structures in the distance. Power poles. The new air has taken fuzziness off the edges of barns and fences. Even without my glasses I can see that the bird on the bush way out there by the front gate is a shrike. I couldn't have seen that four weeks ago.

Last night I woke up at 1:00 a.m. and was rewarded by having to reach for a blanket. The first blanket-reach in the fall is a special thing. It makes you settle into the mattress and relax, in a way that you haven't relaxed since last spring.

The dog went back to the creek with me and barked joyfully about the renewal of that little stream. It's trickling and clear, with pools suited again for splashing into and fetching sticks.

This morning I had to write a check for the October rent. It didn't seem as high as it did in August and September.

"Want to Buy This Place?"

Early Sunday when I drove the five miles into Round Top to get a *Chronicle* at Klump's Grocery I thought I caught a whiff of spring in the air. I sure can't smell it now. Hood of the car's covered with a nice sheet of frost and I was relieved when I turned on the kitchen faucet and got water, instead of that dreaded silent shout that a frozen pipe makes.

But I'm glad to see February being honest. Remember how it suckered so many of us in '87? You know what I was doing almost exactly a year ago? I was right here on this old place, but I wasn't hunkered down by the fire. I was out back stirring dirt with a garden hoe, fixing to put in tomato plants. Because spring had already been here for two weeks.

At least that's what February kept trying to tell us. February can be such a shameless liar. Pear trees were in full bloom. Redbuds flowering. Post oaks popping out their pale greenery. Cardinals singing. Mockingbirds fighting. Sparrows gathering string and grass. Young folks lying around without many clothes on, trying to get their skin color changed before summer.

Then in April, winter suddenly returned and lay a hard freeze over most of the state. My little old garden looked like it had been kissed by a flamethrower. So from now on I intend to remember the rule my country kinfolks used to quote—if we don't have winter in February, we'll have it in April.

The weather up here has become of more concern to me than it was just a month ago, and here's why: In January I was still renting this place, as I've been doing for two years. But now suddenly I am the owner of it. Or anyway I own 50 percent of it, and my partner owns the other half.

Off and on for a lot of years I've been looking for a few acres of woods in this rolling Round Top area, between Brenham and La Grange. But I never could find anything I liked that I could afford. Small acreage, with the features I always wanted, fetch a mighty dear price in this area and I had just about given up.

I remember one hot night last summer. I was sitting with the beer drinkers in Wagner's Store in downtown metropolitan Winedale, just a mile and a quarter from this old house, and we were talking about the difficulty of finding desirable land in small parcels. One of the customers said to me, "Well, if you're waiting for one of these land-owners around here to cut ten or fifteen acres off the corner of his place and sell it to you, forget it because it's not gonna happen. They just don't do it, not unless they're selling to family." And I agreed. My experience told me he was right.

And yet, one morning before last Christmas, my neighbor Charlie Dillingham came across the creek to visit. He owned the land this house is on. He sat down and said, in effect, "How'd you like to buy this place?" I almost fell off the porch.

So Charlie sold us ten acres of woods with the little creek meandering along the north side. And the house, it belonged to Charlie's son George and his wife, Cassie, and they sold us that, and all of a sudden here I am a taxpayer in Washington County. And a house owner, too, and to prove it I've already got a $46.21 plumbing bill from Lloyd Gerland at Carmine.

I just about had to have a partner to help pay for what I've done, or else I'd need to move up here permanently and quit paying rent in Houston. Besides, I've spent enough time on this place to know it's too blamed lonesome without company, especially at night when the owls hoot and the coyotes howl. Hooting owls and howling coyotes make better entertainment if you've got somebody to help you listen.

Beg your pardon for all these details about my real estate doings. But this is the first time in several years that I've owned anything I couldn't pick up and carry off and I'm a little bit excited about it. What I've got to do now is resist going out back and planting tomatoes before winter's over. See you at the post office.

A Very Serious Hole

Dear Boss: I am writing this note to explain why I didn't report to your office yesterday as I promised to do. A little bird came just a few minutes ago and perched on my shoulder and whispered in my ear that you got mighty tired waiting for me and that the strain on your patience has now approached the flash point.

Well, just relax, Boss. You will cool down as soon as I finish giving you the explanation, which is not only entirely satisfactory but interesting and educational, as you will agree.

The reason I didn't show up has to do with a large hole in the ground, and this hole in turn has an important bearing on company business. Does that interest you? I bet it does.

You are wondering, I know, how an ordinary hole in the ground can be related in any way to the health and welfare of a large metropolitan daily newspaper. I will tell you how.

To begin with, this is not an ordinary minor-league

hole. It measures something like 150 feet wide and 260 feet long and is about 14 feet deep. How is that for a serious hole, Boss?

I can hear you asking, "Where is such a hole located?" (Notice that you are showing more and more interest as I go along with this report.)

The answer to your question is that the hole is practically in the backyard of the old country house up in Washington County where I hide out from the telephone on weekends, and sometimes on other days when I seem not to be working, although appearances of that kind are frequently deceiving as you know.

Your next question probably is, "Did the earth cave in and cause this great hole?"

No, no, Boss, it is a *dug* hole, purely intentional. It was dug over the past several days by a Case 450 bulldozer, generating considerable noise and great expense.

"Then the hole has a purpose?" you ask. (Good question, Boss.)

Indeed it does, and this is where the connection to company business figures in. At one end of the hole is an earthen dam, so that this fall when the rains come, the hole will fill and we will have this pretty fish pond.

Can you see it? Around the shores of the pond will be shade trees—live oaks, cottonwoods, and graceful willows. Beneath those trees we'll have picnic tables and comfortable lean-back chairs where people may come and relax and feel the pulse of nature and sip from frosty mugs containing the beverage of their choice.

And fish? You bet. There'll be bass and bream and white perch sticking their heads up, hoping for the honor of being caught. Also white-tail deer will come to drink, and raccoons, and birds of many kinds and hues, and we'll have bullfrogs to serenade us when the sun goes down, and owls to make musical hoots from the trees.

All this, Boss, from just that one hole in the ground.

My part in creating this hole has been to watch it being dug, and pay the fellow who owns the bulldozer that did the digging. He did not finish up quite on schedule, and I was obliged to stay overnight in the country to watch him get through and pay him off, and that's why I didn't report to your office when I was supposed to.

You may ask, "Why was it necessary to watch this hole being dug?"

Boss, you would not ask such a question if you had ever hired a bulldozer, and a man to operate the thing. The cost of dozer work is so extraordinary it's impossible to walk away while that machine is chewing up dollars so fast. You feel compelled to study every little swirl of dust the dozer makes, and try to guess how much money it took to make it. It's something like a guy watching his wife go wild in a jewelry store. It's painful to think about all that money disappearing, but he can't keep from staying there to watch it disappear.

I can hear you asking, "Yes, but I still don't see the connection a stock tank could have with the paper."

Why, Boss, I am surprised. A fellow like you, sitting in such a high place, must surely understand that when one of his hired hands (not mentioning any names) is able now and then to go to a restful place, and restore himself, and listen to the voices of nature, he then will be able to perform his daily duties in a much more efficient and creative manner, and that is good for the paper. Do you see the connection now?

For a complimentary close, let me say what we say up in the country: "May all your vines bear fruit, and may the fire ants not cross your threshold and may all your cows have heifer calves."

The Upstairs View

We have figured out a good way to fix for a Thanksgiving dinner up here in the woods. What you do is call the Round Top Cafe and they wrap up a hot feast—turkey and corn bread dressing and the works—and you drive in and get it and bring it home. The round trip takes fifteen minutes and you're ready to eat. Afterward you burn the paper plates in the trash barrel and there's nothing to wash but hardware. To make things festive and formal we cut a branch of yaupon loaded with red berries and stuck it in a clay pot in the middle of the table.

I violated all the rules of my diet on Thanksgiving Day and did so with a glad and thankful heart. I did it again about an hour ago by eating two pieces of sweet potato pie for breakfast. I intend to start feeling guilty pretty soon, but not until all the pie is gone.

Instead of on the porch, I am sitting in what we call upstairs in the old house. It's a rehabilitated attic. This is the attic that used to be so full of holes the woodpeckers flew through it from east to west without missing a wingbeat. The carpenters came up here and made a pretty good room by raising the roof a couple of feet and sealing up all the holes and adding a few windows. Woodpeckers of all kinds are opposed to sealing up holes and they have been fussing about it ever since the carpenters left.

I am going to like working up here in winter when I can't use the front porch. I'm high, and can look down at the creek behind the house and on north into Charlie Dillingham's pasture. Early in the mornings, when deer season is closed, I can watch a little parade of whitetails move across the pale green ridge of Charlie's hay meadow, way over yonder on the horizon. I haven't seen them lately, not since the shooting season began, but they'll be back.

What I see over there now on the slope are cattle, which belong to Dan Schaeffer, who leases Dillingham's pasture. Seeing those cows makes me feel good. They make a pleasant pastoral scene. What makes me feel good, though, is that I can see them but I don't have to fool with the blamed things. Don't have to feed them or doctor them or chase after them if they get out on the road.

Maybe you have heard cowmen talk about how they love to sit on the porch and look out at their own cattle grazing. What I love to do is sit and watch somebody else's cattle grazing. I can look north and see Schaeffer's cows and I can look south and see Henry Ullrich's cows and that's as near to the cattle business as I want. Having to fool with cows is the reason I went to town and got into the newspaper business in the first place.

About nine o'clock Eugene Hall came from Rutersville to saw up a bunch of timber that was dozed and pushed into piles when we built the fish pond.

Before I met Hall I was about to invest in a chain saw and cut up all that timber myself and burn it in the wood stove. Figured I'd have enough wood for three or four winters. But I talked with half a dozen old dudes who own chain saws, or used to, and they said if you've ever had any back trouble, stay away from a chain saw the same as you would a rattlesnake.

A few minutes ago, after working maybe fifteen minutes, Hall came up from the creek and said that old timber was so hard he had dulled two chains cutting up one tree. "You'd save money," he said, "if you burn that brush where it is, and buy cordwood." So there you are, another curiosity of life in the country in the 1980s. We're sitting in the middle of ten acres of timber and we'll need to buy wood to burn in the stove.

You often run into an old-fashioned code of honor among working people who live in this part of the state, and it tends to surprise Houston folks. Gene Hall, for example. Since his equipment wouldn't do what he'd contracted to do, he didn't want to take any money at all. I offered him money to have his chains sharpened, at least, and to cover the expense of a thirty-mile trip. But he said it was too much.

All my time in Houston has led me to expect a charge of twenty-five dollars for somebody just to come and look, to see if they want to do the work or not.

Some of these permanent folks around here try, I suspect, to keep the Houston people straight on values. Franklin and Kitty Wagner come do things on this place I can't do, or don't want to, and they tell me when to pay again. They'll say, "No, not yet. You've already paid enough."

Now if you'll excuse me I'll go and see if any sweet potato pie is left for lunch.

No Horses, Please

Had a call the other morning from a fellow who offered to sell me a horse. Said he saw in the paper where I had moved to the country, so he thought I ought to have a horse. I don't want any horses, though.

To begin with, I haven't exactly moved to the country. My duties won't let me stay here all the time, so I've been going back and forth, being a sort of half-breed. Part city person and part country. I never have owned a horse, but I know this: You can't just haul off and have a horse. You might think you can, but you can't.

Even if that fellow *gave* me the horse, I would have to

build a fence to keep it from straying. I didn't go to the country to build fence. In my early times, I served a sentence at digging postholes and stretching wire and hammering staples, and I was able to see that I didn't want to do any more of it, ever.

What I am interested in doing in the country is sitting on the front porch. I don't even want a rocking chair, as it requires energy to keep a chair moving back and forth that way. I am deep into a campaign dedicated to the conservation of energy. Sitting still on the front porch is an excellent way to conserve energy. The only better way I know is to lie down.

If I had a horse, granting I went ahead and built that fence, which I am not going to do, next I would have to build a shed. Then I would need to go to town and start buying horse feed and hay.

Then somebody would come along and want to ride. Not me, I don't want to ride as much as a bicycle. But you can't have a horse on the place without somebody wanting to ride it. There'll be friends who know about horses, and they'll say things like: "That horse needs riding. You don't work him, he'll forget what a saddle feels like and go bad on you."

So they'll have me going to town and buying a saddle and a bridle and a blanket. And a rope. Right now I don't own a rope long or strong enough to lead a tomcat to the mailbox.

Then I can hear somebody telling me: "You know this old horse has thrown a shoe? Better get something done about that."

You know what that means. Means you need to take him to the blacksmith, get him shod. True, there are traveling smiths now who'll come to your place and shoe horses, but I know if I had a horse, nobody would come shoe him. Don't ask me how I know that. I just know.

So I'd end up getting a trailer.

You're telling me that's extravagant, that I could always borrow a trailer to get one old horse to a blacksmith one time. Lot of people borrow horse trailers, that's true. Hear 'em talking about it all the time. But not me. I am not allowed to borrow anything with wheels. Heaven has forbid it, or maybe it was hell. If I violate that rule, something bad happens.

You think I'm fooling? I am not. Last time I borrowed a car, not two months ago, I hadn't had it an hour and a half before somebody came along and stole it.

So I'd have to buy a trailer. I'd need it anyway to carry the horse to the hospital. Horses are guaranteed to get something the matter with them and need expensive doctoring. Bankers will loan money to veterinarians with nothing for security except that horses are going to get sick.

Something else I'm not interested in doing in the country is raising crops.

One of my neighbors came by a while back and said he was ordering seed potatoes and wondered if I'd like to get some. Which was thoughtful and I appreciated the offer, but I am afraid to plant potatoes.

Tell you why. It would mean getting out behind the house and spading up a plot of ground. That violates my law of energy conservation. Furthermore, the soil is a nice, sandy loam and easy to work, and that's dangerous. I'm afraid I'd say, well, since I'm planting a few rows of potatoes, I might as well spade up a little more ground and stick in a tomato plant or two. And maybe radishes, because they're easy, and some of those sweet little onions, and I'd end up with the entire backyard planted to vegetables.

When a fellow sets up on even a small plot of ground, people expect him to become some kind of producer. In La Grange the other day, a gent tried to sell me some baby chicks. Said I could raise me some nice fryers. And even before I'd moved in, a friend in the cow business said he'd sell me a couple of heifers.

If I got into all that stuff, I know I would regret it. Along about the Fourth of July, I'd get a call from a friend, and he'd say he could get us into a private lake down in the Brush Country where the bass are big and hungry, so how about let's go down there and spend three or four days hauling in those fish.

I'd have to tell him no. Because my horse is sick, my heifer's about to calve, the deer are eating up my garden, and the coyotes have already got six of my chickens, so I can't go fishing.

That's why I don't want a horse.

IV

CHARACTERS AND CURIOSITIES

Has Anybody Seen Murphy?

At the neighborhood icehouse the regulars often talk about the night Murphy decided to die. I never had the privilege of shaking Murphy's hand, but I have heard the story so often I find myself being surprised that I didn't know him.

A color snapshot of him is tacked to the bulletin board near the cash register. When customers catch a big fish, or kill a deer, or get married, or buy a new car, pictures are often taken and prints displayed on that board. Murphy is there, wearing the new gray suit he bought to die in. As you would expect, in that snapshot he is looking pretty solemn.

I have heard three or four versions of the story. Icehouse stories gain weight as they circulate. But the differences in the versions are mainly in detail, seldom in substance. This is the straight of the matter, the best I could nail it down:

Murphy was forty-eight the night he announced he was going to die. He was also in good health.

He had a daughter somewhere, they said. Her mother died of cancer at thirty-eight and Murphy never stopped hurting about that.

He drank enough booze to flood the streets, for about five years. Then he began tapering off, and finally quit the hard stuff entirely. So he wasn't alcoholic. No alcoholic would taper off that way, do you think? The night he decided to die he drank one beer.

"It was like he just got tired drinking," they'd say about him.

Or "Murphy tried five straight years around here to be a drunk, but he couldn't make it."

He'd come to the icehouse every afternoon, late, and sit around through a couple of beers. If anybody asked him how things were going he'd say, "Pretty well, but I've been missing Sophie today." She'd been gone seven, eight years and he still talked about missing Sophie.

Then he showed up one day at noon and said he was going to die that night. Said he'd be back, later, and tell everybody good-bye.

Sure, it was taken as a joke, at first.

"Hey, did you hear about old Murphy? Says he's gonna die tonight. Yawl better come back by. You wouldn't want to miss Murphy dyin'."

He returned wearing that nice gray suit, with a white shirt and a black tie. New shoes. Everything new. He looked good. He sat off to the side, not with the regulars. He nearly always sat off by himself.

Somebody would come in and see him all dressed up. "Hey, Murph, look at you. You preachin' tonight, or gettin' married or somethin'?"

"I'm gonna die," he'd say.

There would be laughter then and the regulars would work on the idea for laughs. One reason for going to an icehouse is to try to say something that'll make the customers laugh.

"You sick, Murphy?"

"Naw, not sick."

"How you know you're gonna die then?"

"Just know."

"Where you gonna do it? Right here? Can we watch?" Laughter, laughter.

"Naw, I'll go home."

"Hey, Murph, seein' you're gonna die, how about if you give me your watch? That watch ain't gonna run where you're goin'. Be too hot." More laughter.

But the fun didn't last long because Murphy refused to join in. Didn't laugh. Didn't grin. Just sat there solemn as owls, answering questions.

I got two versions of what happened to Murphy's watch. I don't know that the variation is especially significant. One version insists that Murphy took his watch off and gave it to the gent who made the joke about where Murphy would go when he died. Another version says no, he started to but changed his mind, and then got up and said good-bye and went out.

Somebody tried one last joke that didn't work. Yelled at him, "Hey, Murph, I hope it don't hurt much!"

But nobody laughed, and there were no more jokes. The place stayed quiet for a long while. Then one of the regulars asked, "You don't suppose there's any chance Murphy would, you know, kill himself?"

They decided not. One of the ladies said Murphy wouldn't do that because suicide is a sin and if he killed himself he wouldn't get to go where Sophie was.

Somebody raised the question whether a man can just decide to die, and die because he wants to. Indians did it, didn't they? Seen it in picture shows plenty of times. Indian chief gets up from the campfire and says it's time to die and goes out on the prairie and lays down and just does it.

Some of the regulars got worried, felt they ought to do something. Couple of them went to check, see if Murphy was all right.

"He's layin' on his bed," they reported, "still all dressed up. But he ain't dead."

And he didn't die, at least not that night. Some say he came back to the icehouse at noon the next day, looking for his watch. Some say he never came back again, that they saw him around for a while but not at the icehouse. Then he disappeared. Left town, they supposed. Whatever.

Sometimes people show up who say they were present the night Murphy decided to die. Some believe he was playing a spooky joke on the house. Some think he meant to teach them some kind of lesson but they have trouble describing what kind. Something to do with reverence, maybe, like they ought not to make jokes about death. A few think Murphy really wanted to die and couldn't and was ashamed of his failure and that's why he didn't come back.

Then some think he did die, but not quite on the night he picked. One lady (I know she was there on Murphy's last night because she is there all the time) thinks Murphy is dead for sure. She says, "I think he's with Sophie, wherever that is."

Ethel Fell in Love

On Veterans Day I always get a deep hankering to find out whatever happened to certain guys I was in the army with long ago. Some were good guys and some were not so good but they were interesting and knowing them was educational.

Of all those army guys I am curious about, the one I would most like to see now is Red, who was the foremost ladies' man I ever knew.

He was a buck private making fifty bucks a month when I met him at Scott Field, Illinois, in 1943. He had flaming red hair and pale skin with scattered freckles. He was tall and a little too thin.

But there was something out-of-this-world about his face. I can't describe it so you can see him. Just say his face was—well, enchanted, I guess. Whatever it was, it caused girls to love him.

He wasn't real clever or smart and he wasn't what we called an operator who fed them a line of slick talk. I never one time saw him in pursuit of a girl. All he ever did was walk in and grin, and they loved him.

You could ask him, "Come on, Red, tell us, how do you do it? What's the secret?"

He'd say, "Whatta ya mean, the secret?" Like he didn't know what you were talking about.

At parties, for instance. Soldiers then would go to parties at the USO or maybe private homes and girls would show up to dance and get acquainted. A lot of permanent matches originated that way, and tons of temporary ones. Red would walk into a party like that and you know what he'd do? Retreat to a corner, and just sit.

Inside of fifteen minutes you could look over there and

three or four of the prettiest girls in the place would be sitting around him, acting like they wanted to put him in their pockets and take him home.

He stole a girlfriend from me one time. I guess that's why his name comes up here on Veterans Day.

Her name was Ethel, a nice, old-fashioned name. She had big brown eyes and she was a good dancer and she read books and I used to meet her in St. Louis at a place call Tune Town, out close to Forest Park.

Was it Tune Town? Dance Town, maybe. Some of the customers from that part of the country will know the name. I liked that place. Four acres of dance floor and a good big band. It would be called a singles place now, I guess. You went there and hoped to meet somebody significant.

So I had met this Ethel, and we got along pretty well. One Saturday night I told Red where we'd be, because I needed to pay him back a couple of bucks I'd borrowed. We were forever broke and borrowing from one another. Fifty bucks a month didn't stretch too far even in 1943.

He showed up on time at Tune Town, or whatever that place was called, and Ethel fell in love with him before he sat down. I ought to have known better than to expose her to such a danger.

No, he didn't make any sort of move on her. He simply sat there and grinned, and suddenly I was gone. I mean I disappeared, as far as Ethel was concerned, and never existed again. I tried to regain her attention by getting up to dance, and she did appear to go out on the floor with me. But when I got out there she wasn't really present.

Well, I saw what had happened. It would take a half-wit to miss it. Maybe you have known the experience. You sit there with two other people and you're primed to be charming and attractive and nobody will acknowledge that you have even arrived, because there's electrification taking place between those two people. It's interesting and funny to me now, but it wasn't when it was going on.

How it came about exactly I can't remember, but I know when I left that place, Ethel wasn't with me because she was with Red. And when I next saw him, he said that they had gone to her house to meet her folks.

Do you believe that? I didn't either.

But there wasn't any reward in getting mad at him. Nobody ever got mad at him.

Now then, would you spend a minute with me, guessing what sort of adult life that dude has had. Those of us who were defeated by him always thought he was lucky. I'm not so sure now.

The Pleasure of Being Insulted

One of my neighbors walked up to me in the parking lot of the apartment complex where we live and saw I was loading the wagon. He asked, "Where are you off to?"

Told him I was off to attend an insult contest.

"An insult contest? I never heard of such a thing. What kind of contest is that?"

It's just what the name says. It's a contest to see who can deliver the most and best insults. This time we'll have six contestants, and they're all expert dispensers of ridicule, discourtesy, and impudence.

"How does such a contest work?"

We meet at a place we all love, and sit around and swap insults.

My neighbor seemed puzzled. "This is very strange. You must despise one another a great deal."

No we don't. In fact, these are some of the best friends I've ever had, and excellent company. I always look forward to the meetings.

"But why the insults?" my neighbor asked. "Why would six friends get together and sit around insulting each other?"

There. That's the question. I am not sure what the answer is. But an exchange of insults of this kind is common among Texas men, and maybe men everywhere, for all I know.

"What kind of insults are exchanged?" asked my neighbor.

For example, say you have a lawyer in the group. A story will be told on him. It might deal with a widow who wants advice on how to collect a $5,000 life insurance policy her dead husband had. And a week later the insurance company has paid off and the widow gets $500 and the lawyer get $4,500.

"But is that true?"

No, it's not.

"Then I suppose the lawyer gets pretty mad about such a story."

Oh no, he won't get mad. Nobody ever gets mad at one of these contests.

"Why not?"

I don't know why not. One time I attended a meeting of this kind in a small town in this state, and a certain mortician was present. About a hundred citizens were there, all of them prominent business and professional people of the community. A guy got up and told a really bad story on that undertaker.

"What was the story?" my neighbor wondered.

It was about him selling the same coffin over and over. He charged $3,000 for this nice coffin, and it didn't have a bottom in it. When the graveside service was over and everybody left, the body would be lowered into the grave and covered over, but the coffin wouldn't go down with it. It would be put back in the hearse and returned to the funeral home, and pretty soon it would be sold again. Story was that this undertaker sold that same coffin thirty times and made nearly $100,000 off it and built his wife a new house with the money.

"And the story wasn't true?"

No, but it was an interesting story all the same.

"But how did the mortician react to such an insult to his professional integrity?"

He liked it. He got up and beamed and took a bow, and the audience applauded.

"That's weird," said my neighbor.

I know it's weird, but it's common.

"How about you?" my neighbor asked. "Do you get insulted at these meetings?"

Oh yes, all the time.

"How do they insult you?"

They say that I steal. They say that anytime I have a good piece in the paper, it comes from an old book that I've found at a secondhand store, and I just copy it out of that book. Also they say that I seldom work, that it takes me about an hour to type off one of these pieces and then I go to an icehouse and drink beer all day and try to call myself working.

"And that's not true?"

Of course, it's not true. Well, at least it's not *all* true. Hardly any of it, in fact, is true.

My neighbor was really fascinated now. He asked, "Do you, yourself, ever deliver any insults?"

Yes, I specialize in insulting the cook. At these meetings we do a lot of cooking and eating and when the cook makes, say, Irish stew, I like to tell him that I was in jail one time in the Mexican city of Montemorelos and had better stew.

"Is his stew really that bad?"

No, it's excellent stew. But if you brag on what he cooks it embarrasses him something awful, and he may quit cooking altogether. He is not comfortable unless he gets insults.

"Maybe that's the reason for all these insults," my neighbor said. "They may be a form of praise, or an expression of affection. Could that be true?"

Don't ask me about that kind of stuff. All I know is, among this gang attending the contest, a word of friendly disrespect goes over a lot better than praise, which always sounds 100 percent phony.

Neighbor then asked, "Have you ever been made uncomfortable at one of your insult contests?"

I admitted I had, and he wanted to hear the circumstances.

This was back when the meeting first began. Insults were flying. I had never been anywhere and heard as many indignities and affronts.

People in that meeting were shown dreadful disrespect. They were mocked, jeered, offended, taunted. Aspersion was cast on them. They were shown contempt, disdain, scorn, ridicule. I felt terrible.

"Why did you feel terrible?" the neighbor asked. "Did somebody say a bad thing about you?"

No, no. Nobody said a bad thing about me. That was the trouble. I was ignored, which is the worst thing of all.

◆ ——————————— ◆

He Looked Damaged

In New Braunfels I'd made a quick stop at a convenience store, and when I was getting back in the car he honked and waved and motioned that he wanted to talk. A friend I hadn't seen in five years.

You've had friendships like that, I suppose. For ten, maybe fifteen years you'll be close, and talk on the phone almost every week, go fishing together, take trips together.

Then gradually the contact grows less frequent, for no particular reason, and one day it occurs to you that you haven't heard from Tom and Edith in more than a year. You tell yourself, "I ought to call them, see what's going on." But it's late at night when you think of it, or it's too early in the morning, and you put off the calling, and finally you just forget about it.

Five years. I went and sat in his car and we looked each other over and made the standard jokes about hairlines and stomachs. He looked older, sure, but more than that. He looked damaged.

I asked about Edith, and I knew, soon as the words came out of me, that she was gone and this was why his face looked that way—drooped, lifeless.

"It'll be two years, on the sixteenth of July," he said. "Cancer. I don't understand why nobody let you know. I've thought about calling since then, a lot of times, to tell you but—well, truth is, I haven't handled this thing too well. I just wasn't prepared for it."

Which is not the first time I've heard from guys who have lost wives. "Wasn't prepared." They all seem so surprised that, suddenly, after twenty-five or thirty-five or forty-five years, they are without wives.

American humor is heavy with stories about men who practically rejoice when their wives die. How they're out chasing skirts before the grass has grown over the graves of the wives. How they're late for the funeral because of golf dates. That kind of stuff.

Have you ever known widowers like that? Not me. The ones I've known are more likely to be destroyed.

We hear a lot about grieving widows but I think the women deal with losing husbands much better than the men deal with losing wives.

"I thought after a year or two," he said there at New Braunfels, "I'd get better but I haven't. Do you know, there are times during the day when I'm at the office that I forget she's gone, and I pick up the phone to call her?

"And going home, to that house? Sometimes I drive around the block two or three times before I can go in."

Then why not get out of there? Sell the place.

"Well, the kids don't want me to sell it. I don't know if I could do it anyhow. What would I do with all her things? Have a garage sale or something? No way."

Interesting thing is, this was not one of the inseparable couples you often see. Edith would take her tours with some kind of ladies' group. Be gone two, three weeks. Tom used to take three- and four-day trips with me. And he wasn't a husband who felt obliged to call home every night to report where he was and what he was doing. "I need my space, and Edith needs hers," he'd say.

Now he's got all the space there is, and he doesn't know what to do with it.

"Guess what Trisha did not long ago," he said. "Invited me to eat and damned if she didn't have a lady there, a dinner partner for me. My own daughter did that."

Told him I expect Trisha felt after two years it's time for him to rejoin the world.

How about all the usual recommendations the experts make? Church. New activities. Travel. Cultivate friends. Had he tried those things?

"Church I have. You know how Edith used to drag me to church? I go now, every Sunday, but I don't know if I'm going for the right reasons. Probably I'm going just because she always wanted me to."

An idea flickered. I was on my way to the Hill Country for an annual fishing-camping trip I take with friends. How about if he went with me? Just say the hell with whatever he was going to do the next few days. Go get a bedroll and a tackle box and come on to the river with me. Pop a few caps. Watch a couple of sunrises. Might help.

But he wouldn't go. He doesn't want to watch sunrises with me. He wants to watch them with Edith.

"You catch any fish," he said, when I was walking to my car, "stop on the way back and bring us a couple."

Tennyhaw!

Not long ago I spent a short while at a country stag party, never mind where, and I got into a crap game. I didn't stay in it long. Just long enough to lose a polite amount of money.

I confess I enjoy crap games, but not because I win money in them. I never do. What I like is the language of the dice. I always hang around to see if anybody will invoke the name of Sister Hicks, when trying to roll a six. Or if he will know to remind the dice, when he has eight for a point, that Decatur is the county seat of Wise.

Long ago I had an uncle who made a substantial part of his living by gambling. I loved him dearly and believed everything he told me. He used to say it was impossible to make the point of six without help from Sister Hicks. I wanted that to be true. It ought to be.

About the only dice games I see any longer are at country stag parties. These gatherings are generally held on ranches, or in hunting or fishing camps. In the past thirty-five years I bet I have attended as many stag affairs in the country as any guy in shoe leather and I can tell you what goes on at them. The men drink beer, eat too much, talk loud, and gamble.

In fact, the activity at stag events in this state is so

predictable that I have just about quit attending them. It's sort of like seeing the same picture show a couple of hundred times.

But about once a year I enjoy going, to hear the dice talk. I get in the crap game and lose a few bucks as a courtesy. I look at it as a way of paying for the steak I eat. It's not any problem for me to lose at shooting craps. It comes natural.

The other night when the dice came to me I rolled Little Joe, which is a four. In my experience, a four is the hardest point on any pair of dice to make. According to the odds a four is not any harder to make than a ten but I think ten is way easier. In a minute I will tell you why.

As soon as I rolled a seven and crapped out and lost my money, I hung around and watched until somebody came out and got ten for a point. I am always interested in tens.

He was about thirty, wearing faded jeans, a tank top, and a droopy mustache. He had pitched out five dollars and rolled the ten and so, in order to win, he had to roll another ten before he rolled a seven.

Here he came with his second roll and it pleased me that when the dice bounced off the board he shouted the word "Tennyhaw!" He rolled an eight. He got the dice back and hully-gulled them and rolled again. "Tennyhaw!"

Up jumped seven, as they say, so he said an appropriate word and stomped off toward the beer keg, looking real broke. I followed him and found out he comes originally from Hobbs, New Mexico. I asked him if he knows the meaning of that word Tennyhaw.

He didn't. He said his father always said that, when trying to make ten, but had never told him what it means. He said it was just a crapshooter word that goes along with ten, the same as Little Joe goes with four and Sister Hicks with six and all the others.

Then I told him my Tennyhaw story, and he was very interested. My Uncle Barney Hale out in West Texas taught me long ago that in order to make ten in craps, the shooter needed to cry out, "Tennyhaw, Timpson, Bobo, and Blair!" He said these are the names of important towns in East Texas. I'd never been to East Texas then and hadn't heard of any such towns. But I did learn that he was right, that you couldn't make ten without calling their names.

It was curious to me that when I went to Europe in World War II, I would hear soldiers from many states calling these names when they were going for ten in a crap game. I heard guys even from Brooklyn calling them, and if you asked them what the words meant, they wouldn't have the slightest notion.

That interested me, so when I got back home and found a job that would let me roam, I visited those four towns. I've visited them several times now.

Tenaha (often pronounced Tennyhaw locally) is on U.S. 59 near the Louisiana line, in deep East Texas. It's in Shelby County, near the upper end of Toledo Bend Reservoir. Timpson is a few miles away on the same highway. So are Bobo and Blair, which are mainly just rural neighborhoods now and not really towns.

Story I finally got is that the old crapshooter's cry came off the railroad (now Southern Pacific) that crossed the north part of Shelby County. Those four towns were consecutive stops and the conductor's call had a nice alliterative ring. "Tennyhaw, Timpson, Bobo, Blair."

That's the sort of sound a dice player looks for. The first syllable of Tennyhaw suggested the point of ten, and the sounds that followed were rhythmic and satisfying and the cry traveled. From East Texas it went to France in World War I with a company of Shelby County National Guardsmen. How they did spread it!

Thirty-five years later I heard the cry in the hold of a

troopship going to World War II. In Southern Italy I heard it shouted by young men from Pennsylvania and New York and they hadn't any notion they were calling the names of Texas towns. They were just trying to make ten.

Phone Numbers down the Drain

Back home, from being on the road for more than a month. The second I walked in the door I saw that my kitchen drainboard had been scrubbed. It was gleaming, in a state of unnatural cleanliness.

I called up my friend Mel. He has a key to my place and when I leave town for more than a short trip, he comes over and feeds the birds. I have subsidized two litters of cardinals this summer on my little balcony and they are spoiled rotten. They refuse to hunt and peck for food the way ordinary birds do. When the feeder gets empty, they sit out there in the hackberry tree and look pitiful. So Mel comes over and feeds them. If I ever get this flock weaned, I am going to quit feeding birds.

When I got him on the phone, I asked Mel if he had cleaned my kitchen drainboard. He said, "Yes. I couldn't stand to leave it the way it was. That's the only kitchen I was ever in that had socks and underwear on the drainboard and a spare tire leaning against the dishwasher."

That arrangement was only temporary. The spare tire was intended to be stored in the closet before I left town but I was in a press and didn't even have time to put laundry away, much less spare tires. Cleaning the drainboard, however, was unfortunate because it wiped out all the telephone numbers written on it.

"You had phone numbers written on the drainboard?" Mel asked.

Well, yes. I do have notepads by the telephone, but they're always getting covered up by road maps and grocery sacks. So sometimes I write on the drainboard, which has a smooth surface that takes nicely to a felt-tip pen. But now, since Mel cleaned the kitchen, I have lost the numbers of half a dozen parties that I was supposed to call. Did he happen to copy them down before he did his scrubbing?

"No," he said, "I just didn't think of copying down phone numbers off a drainboard. Listen, would you mind answering a personal question?"

Told him to ask it, and then I would decide if I wanted to answer. What he wanted to know was, "Why do you have seven boxes of salt in your pantry. I looked in there for roach spray and you've got seven boxes of salt."

Actually I've got a good many more boxes of salt beneath the sink in the bathroom. He missed those. There is nothing at all strange about that. Four years ago, I was cut loose in the world to make my own way and buy my own groceries. I was shocked by the high price of things. Everything but salt. I liked the price of salt. I could buy a 1-pound 10-ounce carton of salt in the spring of 1980 for twenty-four cents. I couldn't resist it.

What I figured was, the price of salt had to rise. Hoarding salt that way appealed to me. I haven't ever bought anything cheap and held it and sold it for more than I paid. I have always wanted to do that. No, I don't really intend ever to sell salt, but I like to keep track of the market. And I was right about the price. It has gone up. I am now paying thirty-three cents for the same box of salt I paid twenty-four cents for in 1980. I used to have a lot more salt around here than now but sometimes I give it away, as favors, to visitors. Everybody needs salt.

So that explains the seven boxes of salt, but what I wanted Mel to tell me was, what happened to my ten-gallon milk can? When I left town it was sitting by the bird feeder on the balcony and now it's gone.

"Don't worry, I got it over here in my workshop," he said. He's got this nice workshop in his garage. He makes things, and fixes broken ones so that they work again. "You've had that old can for years and never done anything with it. I'm going to strip it and paint it. It'll make you a nice umbrella stand. Umbrella stands made out of ten-gallon milk cans are real popular now."

I told him to hold off. I got that old milk can down at Glen Flora, out of Scheller's Place, my favorite country tavern in all the world. Or anyway it was before it closed. The can belonged to Ed Scheller and if it's painted up fancy it won't ever look like it belonged to Ed. Besides, I don't own an umbrella to put in an umbrella stand.

He didn't understand that position very well, but he did promise not to paint the can. He had a harder time understanding about the old quilt.

Turned out he had taken my old poor-folks quilt. He turned it over to his wife Christina, who sews real well, and she was going to fix these holes in my quilt.

"It's falling apart," he said. "I figured Christina could patch it, and give it back to you good as new."

The trouble is, I don't want it patched. I want it holey. The holes were why I bought it. In my early times I slept 2,000 winter nights under quilts like that. I was kept warm by holey quilts and a hot brick and a brindle tomcat at my feet and I don't want the holes patched.

"All right, all right," Mel said. "I've got your vacuum sweeper, too. I'd better ask you whether you want the pennies and the paper clips taken out of it."

Pennies and paper clips?

"Yeah, that's why it's making all those strange noises. How did you get four pennies and six paper clips into the works of a vacuum cleaner? Do you want me to put them back? Because I've already taken them out."

Sometimes he lets sarcasm creep into his conversation

that way. Still, it's nice to be home and back among friends. While I was gone, I saw some pretty country but I didn't want to move to any of it. The place to be is where people care about you.

Little Emmie

Sometimes I go to a funeral that is not an occasion for mourning but a celebration of a life. I attended one recently up in Brazos County, the funeral of Emmie Pipkin Vick, who was the only mother-in-law I ever had.

She was ninety-seven.

Her grandchildren called her Mimi and many of her relatives and close friends called her Little Emmie because she wasn't quite five feet tall.

I have made a study of Little Emmie's life because I admired the way she lived it.

When she died I hadn't seen her in more than ten years but I kept up with her and toward the end, when she was blind, we swapped a couple of tape letters and I was always inspired by the way her interest in the world never faded.

I believe the last thing she talked to me about was how to cook green beans.

In early summer she would fix snap green beans with new potatoes and there was a trick she had that made this a special treat. I wanted to learn how to fix beans that way but I never found out what the trick was. She said the beans were good because they were fresh out of the garden less than two hours but I think that wasn't the trick. It was something else, secret and mysterious, that was meant to die when she did.

In one of the last letters she also remembered for me the words to an ancient song she sang to my children when they were babies. Song goes:

Weevilly wheat's no good to eat,
Neither is your barley.
Want some flour in a half an hour
To bake a cake for Charley.
Charley is a fine young lad,
Charley is a dandy,
Charley is the very lad
That stole my striped candy.

Little Emmie had a fine, retentive mind. She could sing songs she hadn't thought of in fifty years. She could quote tons of scripture.

She was one of these rare readers who could consume a newspaper from front to back. She was forever asking me questions about why newspapers do certain things and don't do certain others, and often I wasn't able to answer. Because I just hadn't thought of the questions the way she had.

She taught Sunday school in the Baptist church in Bryan for something like sixty-five years. When she was well into her eighties she was driving a little green Plymouth sedan and she would go around early on Sunday morning and gather up what she called "my old ladies" and take them to church and teach them the Sunday school lesson. Most of her old ladies were younger than she was.

She used to scare me, driving that little green car. She depended on God to lead her around and keep her out of wrecks. I wasn't sure God had time to guide a '52 Plymouth over Brazos County and it made me nervous.

All her children were born in a big white house on College Avenue in Bryan. In the fifties, when traffic on that street began to get heavy, she had a hard time crossing it in that little car. She would wait, and wait, and get tired waiting, and finally she'd say, "Well, Lord, get me across because here I go."

And she'd gun across. Did God guide her? Don't ask me that. All I know is, she drove until she was eighty-five without getting hit.

I knew this woman forty years. Her daughter told me at the funeral that Little Emmie prayed for me every night of every one of those years. Maybe that's why I haven't been clobbered on Loop 610.

Some of my habits didn't quite meet Little Emmie's approval but she never lectured me. And we had our little secrets. I was the only member of the clan who didn't mind being seen walking out of a liquor store, and I'd take Little Emmie a bottle of wine that would last two months. I accused her of drinking it out of her thimble.

I admired most the way she dealt with age. I have tried to take a lesson from her.

She'd say, "I have to keep moving." Here's a person ninety-seven years old and blind and she gave herself assignments. She had a day to dust the house. She'd dust, and rest, and dust some more, and this was an all-day job.

Another day she scrubbed. I am talking about an old blind lady scrubbing her bathroom floor. She could have had it done, sure, but she didn't want to. She wanted to keep stirring. Another day she'd wash. And once every week, her daughter took her to the beauty parlor to get her hair fixed for Sunday. Right up to the last, she seldom missed a service in the church where we all gathered the other day to celebrate her life.

Only a few weeks before the funeral, Little Emmie could tell you the price of gold in London. She could talk to you about windfall profits, illegal aliens, Reagan's budget, or nuclear testing. She could talk about Arafat, Khadafy, Jackie Sherrill, or Danny White.

Even when she was lying up there dying, Little Emmie did a special thing for me. She was surrounded by family members, sitting with her all night, doing everything possible to make her departure smooth.

I found out she didn't have flowers in her room because, being blind, she couldn't see them.

So she saved that, for me. I was allowed to send to her room a great lot of flowers, the only thing she didn't have. She couldn't see them but that was all right. She could smell them, and touch them, and she knew who they came from, and said so.

Which was one of the best things she ever did for me.

Listening to J. W.

At our neighborhood icehouse one of the regular customers is an aging gent who is called J. W. He tells a very interesting story about two of his best friends who stole from him a considerable amount of property and cash.

This J. W. is a person of maybe seventy, with nice white hair and lots of seersucker suits and black-lace shoes. About ten years ago his wife died and he was alone in the world except for the friends he has made at the icehouse. Lots of people hang out around icehouses for that reason—they don't care to be alone in the world.

After his wife died J. W. sold their home, which I understand was quite a layout because J. W. has done very well in his business. It has something or other to do with wholesale groceries. When the home was sold, he moved into a condo. He settled in and, as he says, got ready to be old.

"It's very sad to me," J. W. says, telling his story, "that Herman and Lilly would do a thing like that, because they were my friends. We had gone through some hard times together. Herman worked for me, off and on, for almost twenty years and he was always a man you could trust. Lilly came into our home when my wife got to be an invalid and couldn't do the housework. Lilly was a nursemaid to her for more than a year, and it wasn't easy work. But as far as I know, Lilly never said one mean word to my wife in all those months, or did an ugly thing to her.

"Looking back, I knew something strange was going on even before I admitted it to myself. I didn't want to believe Herman and Lilly would steal from me. They were almost like my children. They named one of their boys after me.

"After I sold the house Lilly would come to the condo to clean up, even though I hadn't asked her to. She'd come in and say, 'You can't do for yourself. I worry about you here, all alone.' So she would clean, and cook some, and I'd pay her whatever she asked. It never seemed that she charged very much, and finally I understood why."

J. W. has a little white mustache that jigs and shimmies when he talks. Sometimes it shimmies when he's silent and just getting ready to talk, to tell things that stir his emotions and make his lip quiver.

"There was a period of eighteen months when I wasn't quite in control," J. W. says, going on with his story. "I had that back trouble, and I couldn't get around, and then after my surgery they kept me on those pain pills a lot. And in that time Herman and Lilly stayed at my place and took care of me. I wasn't really capable of doing it myself.

"But I'd have good days when my head was clear, and I'd get up, and try to think about business. I believe the first time I suspected something was going on, it had to do with the garden hose. I looked at an invoice from the hardware store and it showed almost $40 for garden hose. I vaguely remembered Herman saying we needed a hose to water the shrubs on the patio.

"I said, 'Herman, $40 for a garden hose? Isn't that pretty steep?' And he'd say, 'Well, it's good hose.' What he'd do, he'd buy a hundred feet of garden hose and bring one fifty-foot length here and take the other one home. They did that sort of thing, at first. Just little stuff, mostly. Like I'd give Lilly $100 for groceries and she'd go buy $40 worth and manage to forget the change."

His little mustache would be really dancing now, at this stage of the story.

"I wasn't able to prove it—well, I didn't really try to—but I believe they overdosed me on those pills and kept me sort of dopey. I can remember Lilly coming to me with a check to sign. 'For groceries,' she'd say, and I'd sign it and then I'd lay back and I'd try to remember the amount of the check. I'd see it was for something like $500, and I'd think, 'Hey, that's high, for groceries.' But then I'd stop thinking about it. I signed a lot of checks that way.

"What got it stopped, my doctor came to see me. Just dropped in. Said it was a social call. He got me out of bed. Told me to quit taking medicine if I didn't hurt. In a couple of weeks I was a lot better and Herman and Lilly moved back home."

He pauses here, to let his mustache tremble, and to wait for the question. One of the regulars who has heard the story ten times will ask the question.

"How much did they take you for, J. W.?"

"In cash," he says, "around $10,000. They cleaned out my checking accounts. But that doesn't hurt me. I can afford that, and I would have given it to them if they'd asked. What hurt me was what they took beside money. They took a lot of my wife's silver, and her jewelry, and most of her nice things I couldn't bear to get rid of after she died. They even took her plants, her hanging baskets."

Another pause, to get the last question.

"Did you file charges against them, J. W.?"

He clears his throat. Quivers his mustache. "No, I didn't want to. I think eventually they'll prosecute them-selves. Financially they didn't hurt me that much, and a good lawyer would get them off with nothing but mosquito bites."

He then gets up and walks away, looking satisfied. Sometimes I think this awful injustice has become a twisted victory for him, the only thing that's ever happened that makes people listen when he talks.

I have heard the story three or four times and I think it's very sad.

So Long to a Friend

Monday morning I got up early and put on my gray funeral suit and my dark tie and drove to Bellville to say so long to an old friend, Franz Zeiske.

The service was held in St. Mary's Episcopal just off the Austin County courthouse square. This church has one of the most beautiful little sanctuaries I've ever been in, and for Franz's funeral it was full.

I knew it would be. Zeiske was friend to a lot of folks. For most of the years I knew him he was editor and publisher of *The Bellville Times*. After he sold the paper he continued to write a column for it, and he was once a member of the Texas Legislature, so his death drew considerable notice.

During the service I thought about the only other time I'd sat in that church. I was walking around town with Zeiske and when he came to St. Mary's he said, "Let's go in a few minutes, and be still."

That was about two o'clock on an ordinary Tuesday so the church was empty. We sat in a pew near the back and didn't talk. I don't know how long. Several minutes. Just sat there, listening to the silence.

When we went out I felt better some way. I don't

know. Renewed, maybe. The feeling surprised me. I have remembered the incident because it was such a Franz Zeiske kind of a thing. He was a sensitive man, and understood the need of pausing, and being still, and thoughtful.

Something I have found out, at last, is how not to be sad at funerals.

Zeiske helped me learn that. He gave me the first lesson one day when we were driving out of Bellville to Burleigh, just rolling and visiting. A friend of ours had died. Franz made one of his shock statements that he liked to hit you with, to emphasize a point.

He said, "I'm glad John's dead."

What that meant was that John had been hurting a long time with his awful disease and we had been sad while he was suffering because there was no way he could get well. Then at last he was released from his hurting and that was reason to be glad.

I can say the same now about old Franz. He did his share of hurting, so I am glad he's dead.

The rites at Bellville were a memorial service. No casket was present. There was no funeral procession to the graveyard. Franz was a member of the Living Bank, so his body went to a medical institution to be used in research, and possibly for organ transplantation.

That idea appealed to him. He was comforted by the thought that his body, when he died, might help others be healthy and live longer. "The option is," he liked to say, "that you give your body to the worms."

Which was another of his shock statements.

But I mustn't leave the notion that he was harsh. I never knew a more gentle person. If he ever hurt anybody, I would bet he didn't intend to do it. And he was an intellectual, there in Bellville, Texas. A linguist. A reader of classics. A quoter of poems. And a man of great good humor who loved to laugh. When the service was over at the church, I drove out on what we used to call the Old Cat Spring Road, and I did what I promised Franz I'd do.

I parked on the Cat Spring side of the Mill Creek Bridge. On our little rides along the country roads of Austin County, this was one of the stops we always made. We'd leave the car beneath the two black walnut trees and walk down to the creek and watch the water ripple and listen to the birds.

My experience is that most men suffer from the idea that when they die, nobody will come to their funeral. One afternoon I guaranteed Zeiske that if he died before I did, I would not only attend his funeral, I would drive to the Mill Creek Bridge and stand out in the middle of it and take a drink and wish him a swift and happy journey.

So I did it. In my gray suit and black shoes and solid tie, I stood out there and faced upstream and toasted old Zeiske's life, and wished him a happy trip. Maybe it was a peculiar thing to do, with nobody there but me and the crows and the woodpeckers and the robins.

Walking away, I remembered Franz saying that in the deep hole just above the bridge, he once caught thirty-two big crappie, using shiners for bait.

A Late-in-the-Evening Story

One of the customers has asked if I was ever told a good story, and printed it, and then found out the story wasn't true.

I don't believe so, but the question caused me to think of the oyster-eater. I've been trying to bring up his name. The first is Vince, I remember that. The last is the same as a town in Louisiana. Mermentau? Maybe so. Go ahead and call him Vince Mermentau. It doesn't matter much now, anyhow.

I saw him only once. He was sitting in Rick's Place down on Surfside Beach, and he was eating a big plate of fried oysters.

This was back in the early sixties, when I was drifting around the state looking for storytellers. Rick's Place was one of my stops. It was run by Rick and Dewey Rickenbrode.

The legal name of that business was Rick's Beer, Bait, and Beans. I never saw any bait sold there. Nor a can of beans, either, but beans were offered. Three or four cans, wrapped in a thick layer of dust. What the Rickenbrodes sold was beer.

On the night I am talking about, the fellow eating the oysters stirred up my curiosity. How did he rate that service? Dewey Rickenbrode wouldn't have gone in the kitchen and fried oysters for the Queen of England.

"That's Vince Mermentau, the lawyer. He gets anything around here he wants, and he doesn't pay."

The speaker was one of Rick's regular customers. Guy by the name of James something. I didn't know James too well. He was a good talker. I asked him who Vince Mermentau was.

"Well, he's just one of the best attorneys in the country," James said, "and he learned to read right here in this beer joint."

Come on. Learned to read?

"That's right. I was in here the first night Vince came to the beach. He jumped a French freighter up in Houston and wandered around in that Turning Basin neighborhood a few nights, and got his money taken away from him. He thumbed his way out of Houston, sort of running from trouble. Walked in here hungry and Mrs. Rick fed him, gave him a place to sleep, and he hung around."

That last, about Dewey Rickenbrode feeding a stranger,

that made sense. She was always taking in beach bums, feeding them, loaning them money. Taking them to doctors. Unrecorded charity, that's not deducted from income tax.

"Mrs. Rick let Vince do little jobs," James said. "Sweep. Fix things. He could speak a few words of English but one day we found out he couldn't read."

Couldn't read English?

"Couldn't read any language. Can't read French even now. He was just flat illiterate. Smart? Smart as anybody, but where he came from, he just hadn't been taught to read."

So how did he learn?

"Mostly from the funny papers," James said. "One night he came up to Mrs. Rick with the Sunday funnies and asked her what the words meant and after she read them she said, 'You know what we ought to do? We ought to teach Vince to read.' So we did."

Using just the comic strips?

"At first, yeah, but then he got into trying to read the news, and he pretty near drove us all crazy around here, asking questions about words, and how to spell them and all.

"Sort of in self-defense, the regular customers would teach him. We got to bringing him books. Some of the women brought him children's books, and some brought old books they had in attics and hadn't read since they were kids, and we'd have a reading class here, for Vince.

"It was the opposite of school, where you have one teacher with twenty-five students. Some nights we'd have twenty-five teachers and one student, just Vince. It was a project for us. Hell, we were proud of him. Inside a year he was reading books on the best-seller list."

But how about this lawyer business?

James said, "After he'd been around here a couple of years, Vince had read twice as much as any of us who taught him. He got one of those high school equivalent diplomas, and went to Brazosport College, and swallowed everything they had in a year and a half, and started talking about going to law school.

"So we sent him. We pitched fish fries and barbecues, and we raised the money and we got him in that law school in Houston and he came out tops in his bunch.

"Now he's got an office in Freeport and he's making good money. Anytime people here on the beach have got legal problems, Vince takes care of them and there's no charge, and never will be. About once a week he comes down here to check on Mrs. Rick, and he gets whatever he wants.

"I'm surprised you haven't heard about his big lawsuit. With the shrimpers? Some complicated thing about international waters. Vince says it may go to the Supreme Court. If it does, we're gonna charter a bus and go up there and listen to him argue. Our personal lawyer, who couldn't read when he walked into this place and here he is talking before the highest court in the land."

James got up then and left, with a six-pack to go. I went over to Vince's table.

I asked about the lawsuit with the shrimpers and he didn't know what I was talking about. He said he worked on a shrimp boat out of Freeport and was born in Louisiana's Calcasieu Parish. He had shucked a gallon of oysters that day and brought them to Mrs. Rick as a gift and that's why she had fired up her skillet for him.

You've got to watch storytellers close, because some don't mind saying what's not true. An especially risky place to hear a story is in a tavern on the beach, late at night.

La Bruja Carinosa

At the neighborhood icehouse I heard a story about Catalina, who calls herself La Bruja Carinosa (The Benevolent Witch). The story tells how Catalina could forecast events and locate lost items of significant value.

I am not certain that all the stories told at the icehouse are totally factual, but that doesn't keep them from getting an attentive audience. The one about Catalina involves a gent called Woodrow. He has a last name, but I was not able to hear it clearly. Last names in icehouses are apt to be muttered, and nobody is ever willing to spell one for you, especially not if you are holding a pencil and threatening to write the name in a notebook. Woodrow had lost his job, a circumstance common among icehouse regulars now. When this happens, the victim of the layoff is apt to become very popular on a temporary basis because he often receives severance pay and carries for a little while a lot more cash than he ever did when employed.

The story goes that Catalina drifted around to Woodrow's place one Sunday morning and asked to borrow a cup of sugar. While Woodrow was looking in his pantry for sugar, Catalina put her hand to her forehead and spoke these words:

"Your telephone is about to ring."

"How do you know?" wondered Woodrow.

"I can hear it," said Catalina. Her face suggested she was in moderate pain. Her voice grew faint, mystic. "I see the caller. It's your Cousin Harvey, who has good news."

"No way," said Woodrow. "If it's Harvey, it'll be long distance and collect, and that's not good news." He went on looking for sugar.

Then to Woodrow's great surprise, his phone rang and

it was Cousin Harvey calling, long distance and paid, to say he was sending Woodrow the fifty dollars he'd borrowed a month before.

Monday morning, Woodrow was astonished when the promised money came to him by express mail. He went to Catalina and said: "You're fantastic. How do you know these things?"

Catalina still seemed mystic, distant. She pressed a hand to her forehead again and said, "I see your stolen money belt."

"But my money belt has not been stolen," Woodrow said.

"Well," said Catalina, "I see *somebody's* money belt. It has $500 in it, and it's hidden under a plank on a vacant lot near your house."

That statement got Woodrow's attention because, when he was laid off, he put $500 of his severance pay in a money belt and hid it under his mattress. He rushed home, turned the mattress. The money belt was gone. In desperation, he ran to the only vacant lot on his block. In the grass lay a rotten board. Woodrow lifted the board and found his money belt, with every dollar of the $500 still in it.

He returned to the house of Catalina to thank her for knowing, in some miraculous way, that his money had been stolen. He offered her a fifty-dollar reward. She refused.

"It is bad luck to take money you don't earn," Catalina said. "If I wanted such money, I could have gone to the vacant lot and taken the $500 from beneath the plank. Is this not so?"

Woodrow saw that this was so. "Have you seen hidden money very often?" he asked Catalina.

"Many times," she said. "I know of $10,000 hidden in a barn in the state of California. It is money from a bank robbery."

"Why don't you go there and get this money?" Woodrow asked.

"Because I don't want it," Catalina said. "Besides, to go there would cost a great deal and I am a poor woman."

"How much would you need?" asked Woodrow.

"Too much," said Catalina, sighing. "Maybe $2,000. It is impossible."

"It's not impossible," Woodrow said. "We may be able to make a deal." And so he convinced Catalina that she could go to California and return with the money, and the two would split it. To cover expenses Woodrow gave her $2,000, which was all his severance pay and more.

This was almost a year ago, and as far as anybody at the icehouse knows, Catalina is still in California after the money. Some have mentioned a story they heard from a truck driver, who said he saw Catalina in San Antonio last Cinco de Mayo in company with Woodrow's Cousin Harvey.

And some say Catalina will not return, ever, and that Woodrow will never get his money back. Or the cup of sugar, either.

A Nice Set of Directions

We were on the driveway of a gas station in Huntsville and this gent was giving me directions on how to find a certain piece of property in the country. He said:

"Go on west this away on your first blacktop and turn north. That'll be to your right. That road carries you, oh, two, three miles back in there. You'll come to a bunch of trailer houses and a fellow that keeps white chickens. You'll see those chickens. Sometimes they're out on the road. Tuesday I run over one. A good half mile past the chickens the blacktop plays out and there's a fork and some mailboxes. You want to bear west. That'll be to your left.

"From there on, just take all your rights for something like a mile and three quarters till you top a little rise and come to a tin barn and a house with chinaberry trees. Nobody's at the house but there'll be a black and white dog laying in front of the gate. The ground you're looking for is the piece just north of the barn. It's twenty-five acres and it's a wedge. Wide part's at the back, along the creek, and the front comes to the road and corners at the barn. There's a gap but I wouldn't try to drive down to the creek. I'd go afoot. That low ground's still pretty wet, all this rain.

"You get through, you don't have to come out the same way you went in. You can go on north. It's a mile or two longer back to town but it's pretty country. Lot of dogwood out. When you cross the creek above my place, road goes off in about three directions but you'll see a set of old pens and all you do, you keep those pens to the north of you. That'll be to your left. You'll have another fork up there I guess three miles after you cross the creek and if you turn wrong there you might get lost. But not for long, and it ain't gonna hurt you. At the fork, bear east. That'll be to your right."

Out of curiosity I asked how he knew the black and white dog would be at the gate and he said, "That's my dog and I know where he stays. He won't hurt you, but don't fool with him."

I liked that speech and I took notes on it. Then a little way out on the road I stopped and wrote the speech out in detail, the best I could remember it. Not just so I'd have the directions. Sometimes words like that, spoken by rural people about things that are ordinary to them, have rhythm and character and they're worth writing down and saving.

The directions worked fine. The trailer houses showed up on schedule and so did the white chickens. I checked my odometer and measured to see what he was calling a good half mile. Figured out at a little better than six-tenths. About right, I thought.

The mailboxes were at the fork and I bore west, which was to my left. The reason he kept saying right and left, it was a courtesy. Rural people have learned that city folks asking directions in the country are not apt to know east from west. But it's natural for compass points to be used in the country, and givers of directions often interpret them. It saves you having to ask whether turn east means left or right.

I have found Houston people who don't know what it means for a blacktop to play out. It just means the pavement ends. The term blacktop was not common in Texas in my early times, since so few minor roads were hard-surfaced then. The name is applied now in the country to all asphalt-paved roads except the major ones. A federal or interstate highway, paved with asphalt or not, would never be called a blacktop. Blacktops are generally farm-to-market and country roads.

There's a wry joke about the fine network of blacktops this state has built since World War II. Farmers say when they needed the roads was in the twenties and thirties and early forties, because they were out there a foot deep in mud. Now that they've got the roads, all the farmers have moved to town and don't need 'em. Which is an exaggeration but not much of one. Maybe a greater irony is that now the city folks are swarming over the farm roads and buying up the land and moving out there where the farmers used to live.

Everything was just as the gent in the gas station said. The tin barn and the house with chinaberries and the black and white dog in front of the gate. I liked his sentence about that dog. "He won't hurt you, but don't fool with him." What that means is, "If you fool with him—harass him, or even try to pet him—he very well *might* hurt you."

He said there'd be a gap, so I could go through the fence and walk across the property to the creek. A gap, as some may not know, is an opening, usually in a barbed-wire fence. It serves as a gate. It's simply a part of the fence that can be opened and shut.

He was sure right about the ground being wet near the creek. A car would have settled directly to its frame. So I went in afoot, as he suggested. I like that, afoot. I seldom hear the word used in cities any longer.

I kept the set of pens to my left and went the long way back to town. A set of old pens? That means abandoned cattle pens, or corrals, used in working cattle, branding and marking and spraying and vaccinating. Old corrals like that are all over this state and they become reference points, landmarks.

Somewhere on the way back to town I turned wrong and got lost, as he said I might. He also said it wouldn't hurt me because I wouldn't be lost for long and he was right about that, too. In fact I didn't stay lost as long as I wanted to.

Wildflowers and Pinto Beans

The prettiest wildflowers I've seen this spring along a highway are between Fredericksburg and Mason. It's a great year for prickly white poppies. On that Fredericksburg-Mason highway the poppies sometimes make the pastures look like fields of open cotton.

The best bluebonnets I've seen are growing in a place

I never expected them, and in one sense that's too bad because very few folks will get to enjoy them. They're blooming in an outrageous way along several miles of a dirt road west and south of Mason. It's the county road we use to reach our James River campsite here on the Schulze Ranch.

I think of this land as being fairly rugged. I doubt you would insult it if you called it semidesert. It's rocky and covered mostly by small mesquite and squatty brush.

This spring it has exploded into bluebonnet flowers.

I grew up on land like this, but I never before saw rocky, brushy hillsides covered with bluebonnets. Blossoms so thick they seem artificial. Once I stopped, on the road coming to camp, and burned some color film on six mesquites growing knee-deep in bluebonnets. The color in places is so intense the land seems to heave in blue and white and pink waves. I wish you could see it.

A year ago when we were here, this country was hurting for moisture. Since then the rain has come, lots of it, and the land responded with all this greenness and all these blossoms. It's like the rains they talk about in pure deserts farther west, where no moisture comes for ten years. And then, when it does, the desert produces spectacular flowers and people living there might see this only half a dozen times in their lives.

We camp here on a great flat rock where I'm sitting now. Near me is a layer of coarse gravel deposited by the river when it was on a roaring rise not long ago. Out of that gravel, five bluebonnets have sprouted and bloomed. It's like the land is saying, "Give me water, and I'll produce beauty out of stones."

We've been coming here to this rock on the James River several years. Right now we are four. The others are off fishing, and I won't see them until the pinto beans are done. They are John Graves of Glen Rose, Bill Shearer of Fredericksburg, and Glen Bass of Tyler. Then there's an

Old English sheepdog called Hodge, belongs to Graves. Hodge is bored by fishing and is here with me in camp. A good dog with nice manners.

I volunteered to stay in camp and cook beans this morning. I pretended it was a sacrifice, but the truth is I needed the solitude to get this report done. Also I like being here, just me and ol' Hodge, cooking beans and listening to the music of the river and the birds and the wind. I feel good here.

Always have. I've never come here that I didn't end up feeling better than when I left home. In fact, I did an extraordinary thing on this river. One time I came with the flu, running fever, and I sat here and honestly felt good. My flu wasn't cured, but I was able to feel fine while having it. Now then, how do you account for that, Doctor?

I have invested a lot of myself into these beans. I want them to be good. I want them to be bragged on. I want somebody to say, "Best beans ever cooked on a river bank and stirred with a screwdriver." I may say that myself if nobody else does.

The reason I'm stirring with a screwdriver is that Fred Whitehead hasn't showed up yet. He is the other charter member of this expedition. He comes out of Austin, bringing such luxuries as little gasoline stoves and knives and forks and plates and Crisco and cornmeal. And a cook spoon, which we won't have until he arrives, so I am stirring with a nice long screwdriver I found in my spare-tire well.

Now and then this Hodge dog gets up and shakes the debris out of his shagginess and comes over and looks at what I'm doing, as if he wants to correct my spelling, or suggest a fresh verb. We sit close together a while and appreciate the sounds. A canyon wren running down that part of the musical scale it knows. A cardinal. A bobwhite quail. Killdeers. Frogs. Occasionally a wild turkey, gobbling upstream where the timber is thicker. All satisfactory sounds.

I am fixing way too many beans. Four pounds, dry weight. But I brought my great restaurant-kitchen pot, and you can't, with any grace, cook two cups of beans in a pot this big. Two cups would insult it. The beans are coming along, but they lack something. Wish I had an onion about the size of a Pecos cantaloupe.

Did I mention the yucca blooms? They are on the face of the cliff across the river from camp. Graves says sometimes when he's fishing he gets the feeling somebody is watching him. He'll turn to look, and it's those big yucca blooms. From a distance they do give the image of big creamy-white faces, staring out of the brush. We are talking about a plant sometimes 14 feet tall, making a cluster of flowers 2 feet long and 10 inches wide. From this rock I count ninety-three of them across the river.

The beans are getting better, but they still lack character. I am thinking of pouring two cups of red wine in them. What do you think?

Sick on the Road

Many years ago when I first started out in the column-writing business, I had an editor who told me that I ought never, ever, to miss filling my space on the day I'm supposed to fill it. He insisted he could not think of a good reason for a columnist to miss a day.

Not having anything to write about, in that editor's view, was the worst excuse of all the dozens he had heard. Even a death in the family wasn't excuse enough for him. Neither was being sick.

"If you get sick," he said, "write about how sick you are."

I have done that a good many times across the years and here I am doing it again. Right now I'm in a motel room in the city of Hearne, and feeling entirely blitzed. Some bug or other has got hold of me.

The reason I came up this way, I was going to visit a nice haunted house that some of the customers have been telling me about. It is evidently just loaded with ghosts who make all manner of interesting sounds. The house is not right here in Hearne. I am not telling where it is, just yet.

I had to scrub the haunted house mission on account of this bug that's got me. I am not fit to visit in anybody's house, haunted or not.

Being sick on the road is a drag. The only good place to be sick is at home where you can be comforted by your own pillows and quilts, and have access to the personal pharmacy in your bathroom medicine chest.

Some people who travel a lot carry their medicines along. I know traveling guys who carry pills and ointments for a dozen different ailments, all the way from hangovers to the heart trouble they don't have but evidently expect to get.

I never have carried a drugstore like that. To me it reflects a negative attitude. I prefer to imagine that I will be able to travel from Houston to Hearne and back without the need of medical treatment.

Yet here I am in Hearne, sick. I am telling you about this because it makes me feel better. Sick on the road is a lonesome business.

Also I'm vaguely comforted that I can recall times when I was a lot sicker on the road than I am now.

One time I wandered off down in Mexico to work. First night I stopped at Valles and somehow got acquainted with the fellow who managed the restaurant in the hotel where I bunked. He wanted to talk about the food of Mexico. He was distressed because when Texans came to Mexico, they expected all the natives to be eating nothing but tortillas and chili con carne.

I got him to order me what he thought was a good meal for a Texas tourist in Valles. He sent out a nice hunk of beef with a dark sauce and a great handful of mushrooms. Which was okay. What got my attention was the salad. Its principal ingredient was green squash, raw.

I could see the rule for American travelers in Mexico: Avoid eating uncooked fruits and vegetables unless they are peeled.

But how are you going to avoid raw squash in a salad when the fellow who is proud of it stands there watching you eat. I ate everything, and it tasted fine.

Three days later in Mexico City I was sick as a yellow dog. Three more days later I was in Guadalajara and still sick. I told the desk clerk at the hotel to find me a doctor. He asked my symptoms and I told him. He gave me the name of a druggist, not a doctor.

Off I crept, my illness diagnosed by a desk clerk. I finally found the druggist. He was in a little stall in a market, with piles of pineapples and hanging cow heads. And a great stack of fresh squash. I walked way around it.

He sold me one tablet. Or maybe I ought to call it a wafer. It was a thin white disk, about the size of a half dollar. Was that all? Just that one tablet?

He said gravely, "You won't need another one."

I carried that thing back to the hotel and tore it up into half a dozen pieces and took it with a Bohemia. By that time I was afraid to drink water down there, even when I saw it poured out of an Agua Puro bottle. Then I went to bed.

About 2:00 a.m. I woke up in the grandmother of all

sweats. I wouldn't have been much wetter in swimming. I kept sweating like that, off and on for twenty-four hours. When it was over, I was well. Weak as a schoolboy's excuse, but well.

What was in the tablet only God and that Mexican druggist know. I thought about going back to ask him but something told me just to let it go and I did.

My friend Mel has a sad sick-on-the-road story about him and his wife Christina. One time for an anniversary present, he took her to New York.

That's what she asked for, a week in Manhattan, to stay in a ritzy hotel, eat in fancy restaurants, see the plays, all that stuff tourists do in New York. Mel swallowed hard and delivered. He hates getting on airplanes and hates paying the check in expensive restaurants. But he went, since it was Christina's request.

Time they checked into the hotel up there, Christina was sick with a stomach virus. She stayed in wretched condition the whole week. Mel sat by her bed and fed her crackers and Coke. Neither of them saw a play or went into a restaurant. When she got out of bed, all she wanted to do was go home.

A sad story. They might as well have been in Hearne, where I am feeling a little better.

Rushing the Season

Half a dozen of the regular customers at the neighborhood icehouse had moved outside, to the picnic table beneath the pecan tree where they spend the summer. Rushing the season, because the wind was raw and unfriendly. They do that every spring—sit outside before outside is ready for them.

But they stayed, and made a curious scene. Six people, huddled into coats and jackets, sipping suds from frosty bottles.

The one called Pauley drained his longneck, signaled for another, and delivered the following address:

"This always makes me think of early in the spring when we were kids, and the way we'd sit on the bank of the creek and wait for the water to warm up enough to go swimming. Used to play hooky and do that. Just stare at the water, like if we looked at it another twenty or thirty minutes it'd be warm and we could all jump in.

"The month of March, you stuck much as a finger in that creek it'd pretty near freeze, water's so cold. But we liked to go anyhow, and look, and talk about the fancy dives we'd do soon as we could swim. In March we were all daredevils. We'd promise to do anything, long as we didn't have to do it until May.

"At the hole where we swam, there was a big old tall cottonwood, must have been a hundred feet or better. Wait a minute now, it wasn't a cottonwood. What's that tree's got the slick white bark?"

Somebody said sycamore.

"Sycamore. Bark so slick a coon couldn't climb it. We'd bring short boards, like rungs on a wooden ladder, and nail 'em to the trunk so we could get up in there and dive off. We had a rope swing, too, tied high in the tree and you could get way back on the bank and swing out on the rope and let go."

A fellow standing behind Pauley said, "Did you have a trolley, too, that stretched across the creek?" He had just wandered up, and got tuned in to the speech. Three or four others were standing with him.

"Damn sure did have a trolley, that's right," Pauley said, turning, pleased to discover strangers being interested, talking louder to include them. "Trolley was a cable, from one of those old abandoned rigs. It came out of the top of that big tree and then slanted over the creek to a stump in the edge of the water on the other side. A pipe maybe a foot long was on the cable and you hung on to that and slid down and let go when you got out over deep water. Sometimes we'd get axle grease, and grease the cable and, man, that baby'd slide down sixty to nothin', scare the shorts off you.

"But daredevils, I'm telling you in March when the water was still cold we weren't afraid to do *anything*. An old boy'd say, 'You know what I'm gonna do, first day we can swim? I'm goin' off that top limb up yonder, head first. Do a swan dive.' That old cottonwood, I mean that syca-more, had one big limb way up, close to where the cable was tied. Very few guys had the sand to climb up there and dive. All of us'd *say* we'd do it, in March or early April, but when the water warmed up that limb looked higher 'n the courthouse. I climbed up to it one time and looked down. Man, you couldn't pay me all the money in that First National Bank to dive off there.

"Sometimes, playing hooky to go look at the water, we'd overdo. I mean too many of us would cut out of school the same afternoon. My Lord, you'd have half the arithmetic class on the creek.

"We had an old boy, Mr. Reinhardt, for principal then. Pretty good old squarehead, really, but we were all scared of him. And he was hard to outsmart.

"One time when a gang of us was playing hooky, we had enough to hold a pep rally. Must have been twenty-five guys, sitting in the sun about 1:30 in the afternoon. All of a sudden Old Man Reinhardt walked up and caught us.

"He didn't say a word, at first. Just walked through

us, real slow, looking at everybody like he was taking names. After a while he squatted down and stuck his hand in the creek, and sort of swished it around. Then he got up and he said, 'Boys, I'd say this water's not gonna be ready for another two weeks.'

"That's all he said, and he walked away. Every one of us followed him back to school. I wish now I had a picture of that, of Old Man Reinhardt walking away from the creek with twenty-five of us following along behind him like a bunch of sheep."

The Hitchhiker

Last Tuesday morning I was rolling down Texas 36 south of Brenham and wasn't in any kind of hurry so I turned off the main road and went into downtown Kenney. You've been to Kenney whether you know it or not. It's a nice little town on 36 about halfway between Brenham and Bellville. Truckers and roving reporters and wandering minstrels and everybody else who traveled regularly along Texas 36 used to talk about Kenney on account of its underpass. The highway did a lot of snaking and went beneath the Santa Fe tracks through a narrow underpass, and it could be exciting if you tried to make those curves too fast.

The underpass remains, but the highway goes around downtown Kenney now—and for that reason I hadn't stopped there in several years. Tuesday morning when I did, Elmer Freitag was standing out front of his general store on the main drag.

That made me feel good, to drive into town and find Elmer standing there with a couple of rolled-up newspapers under his arm. Freitag's Store used to be one of my regular stops when I was trying to get acquainted with every country storekeeper in this state. I didn't get around to them all, but I made a pretty big dent in the total.

My theory was that country storekeepers as a general class are smart citizens and if I talked to enough of them, I would get pretty well educated. Actually, that was my father's theory. He used to say that anybody who dropped a hoe and walked out of the cotton patch and went up on the road and opened a store had to be smarter than the ones who stayed in the field.

"Look at Walter," he'd say. He meant his brother, my Uncle Walter Hale, who operated a country store at Oakwood for many years and accumulated a good deal more in his life than his brothers did. I had the chance to hang around that store and listen to Uncle Walter talk, but I didn't do it much. I wish I had now.

Elmer Freitag there at Kenney had one of the really good general stores in Texas. He also operated the Kenney post office in the back of the store. He is retired now.

While Elmer and I stood talking, I had the front door of the car open, and a black and white cat came nosing around and hopped up on the seat. Elmer wanted me to see the new Kenney post office. So I put the cat out of the car and shut the door, and we went to look.

Personally, I always liked post offices in country stores. There was something appealing about a postmaster who would sell you not only the three-cent stamp but also ten pounds of potatoes and a gallon of lard. Most of the country store post offices are gone now.

An interesting thing is, that sort of post office is showing up in the cities. Little substations, in the backs of drugstores. There's one on Fountainview in Houston, and last Christmas I discovered another out on Richmond where I mailed a bunch of packages in a fraction of the time it would have taken in a regular post office. But I'm wandering off the subject.

The new Kenney post office is in the brick building where the bank used to be, and it's a nice setup. We inspected it, and then I shook hands with Elmer and drove on south to Bellville. I stopped to buy gas, and then drove out on Mill Creek Road to see the new bridge they've built on the creek. I loved the old one. It was an iron bridge that made music and I wish they hadn't torn it down. Next I stopped at the Crossroads Tavern at Cat Spring to use the telephone. I am telling you about all these stops for a special reason.

From Cat Spring I went out to John Blocker's ranch on a matter of business, and from there I drove up to New Ulm hoping to get Alton Haverlah at the Parlour to tell me a war story. Alton is full of World War II stories and can tell them in English or German. But on Tuesdays the Parlour doesn't open until four o'clock, which I knew but had forgotten. So I went to the filling station and tried to call E. P. Stallings at Fayetteville, in the hope that he would ask me to come spend the night. But he had gone to Houston on business.

Well, when I opened the door to drive on, that black and white cat was sitting on the back of the seat over on the passenger side.

Evidently it had hopped back in the car when Elmer and I went into the post office at Kenney and had ridden along with me without making any comment. It wasn't complaining. Just sitting up there licking its foot and looking at downtown New Ulm.

There wasn't anything to do but deliver that cat back to Kenney because a lot of people place a great value on cats and will enter into serious grief when they get carried off. So I returned to Kenney. When nobody was looking, I eased up to Freitag's Store and unloaded the cat on the sidewalk and drove away.

Since then I have been thinking about that cat, and something is bothering me. I have the feeling that when I put that animal out, it looked bigger than it did before it took the ride with me. Do you suppose it wasn't the same cat? Could it have got in the car at one of those later stops?

If anyone is missing a black and white cat in Bellville, or out on Mill Creek Road, or around Cat Spring, or New Ulm, all I can do is suggest you start looking for it at Freitag's Store in Kenney.

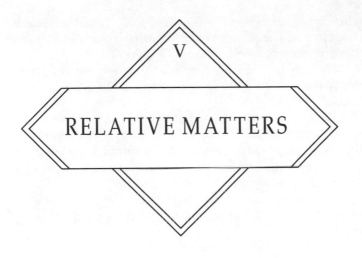

V

RELATIVE MATTERS

Dirty Tricks

Here is a Christmas card from Cousin C. T., who writes a note to ask if I remember the time I put the dead rat in his Christmas stocking.

C. T. was one of my country kinfolks back in our barefoot times, and he was forever working wicked and painful stunts on those of us who were younger or slower-witted than he was.

He says on the card that in the mellow years of his life, he does a lot of reflecting and he is shocked by the memory of all the outrageous tricks his loved ones played on him back when he was "an earnest and well-mannered boy."

I'm surprised the paper he wrote that phrase on hasn't

withered beneath the words. Because C. T. was a devious boy. He made a specialty of doing dirty tricks and blaming them on somebody else. He was expert at it.

He was the one who dropped the kitten into the churn when it was full of buttermilk, and credited that stunt to me.

He was the one who advised me that the way to un-saddle a skittery horse was to leave the gate open and take the bridle off first. The result was a saddled horse, without a bridle, heading off into the pasture at a high lope, in view of the adults sitting on the front porch.

C. T. was the one who guaranteed that if I stood bare-footed in a red ant bed, no ant would sting me if I held my breath.

Despite these and worse atrocities, I admired C. T. and followed him everywhere. He was older and bigger and seniority in those times meant everything.

I admired the lies he made up. Like the one about the sins in the stock tank. This tank was a small pond where we went swimming. After brush-arbor revivals, the converts were sometimes brought to that stock tank and baptized.

Cousin C. T. explained to me that this meant their sins were washed away and if I didn't believe it I could read it in the Bible. He said further that all those sins were wiggling around there in the tank and if I went out in the water about waist deep and stood still, I could feel them start to nibble on my feet and legs.

He said you couldn't drown a sin. He said a sin would wash off a sinner but it didn't die—it floated around looking for somebody else to get onto. The thing to do, he said, was never to stand still in the water. If you kept moving, the sins couldn't get hold of you.

Sure, I knew better than to believe such a thing. And yet, I could feel the sins nibbling at my hide when I was still in the water. I suppose they were minnows or polli-wogs or tadpoles but they felt like sins to me and to this day if I stand in a lake or a creek and feel nibbles on me, I think of Cousin C. T.'s lecture on baptism and where the sins go.

Did I ever tell you about the time C. T. streaked, all the way from the barn to the grape arbor, in the middle of the afternoon? He was the original streaker, at least in my experience, and I admired that he was willing to assume the risk.

The size of the risk was mountainous. The path of the streak was in clear view of the house, which was full of women and girls. If he had been seen, C. T.'s father would have—well, I wonder whether that stern farmer could have thought up a punishment severe enough for such a crime.

I believe C. T. felt that running naked across that sandy stretch of ground showed not only courage but a sort of nobility, as well.

Years afterward, it occurred to me that I missed an opportunity that day to pay C. T. back for all the mischief he'd done me. Because I had him in a vulnerable spot. Before he made the streak, he sent me to hide beneath the grape arbor and wait there with his shirt and overalls and underwear.

I could have disappeared, and hidden his clothes, and left him stranded, naked, and this would have served him right. But I didn't think of it.

That night at supper C. T.'s father asked us a routine question. "What kind of nonsense you boys been up to?" And C. T. answered, his face stiff and his eyes blank, "Nothin'. No kind at all."

I suppose you can see, from that background, that it wasn't me who put the dead rat in C. T.'s Christmas stocking. It was the other way around.

Footlog Adventure

Something I'm interested in is footlogs, for the reason that they were our first bridges. Here came a storm or a flood and a big tree fell across the stream and when the water receded, there she stood, a way to cross the creek without getting wet.

Then the first man-made bridge followed, patterned after the natural one. Somebody cut down a tree in such a way to make it fall across the creek. Then maybe they trimmed and smoothed the top of the log, to make a better walking surface.

Long ago up in Palo Pinto County I used to knock around the bottoms with my Cousin C. T. after we'd have big rains and creek rises. It was wonderful to discover all the changes that a rise had brought to the streams. Here would be the trunk of a great oak spanning the stream, an excellent natural bridge provided free of charge.

Footlogs like that, new ones, meant adventure because they had to be crossed. You couldn't just have a footlog. You had to go across it, and you had to do it standing up or it didn't count.

Footlogs with the limbs and foliage still on them sometimes provided a challenge, and taught you things about yourself that you didn't know. Things like how quick you could make decisions, and the basis you used to make them.

Here's an example I remember:

You've picked your way more than half across a new footlog, holding onto projecting branches and weaving among the twigs and leaves. You reach out to brush aside a branch that's in your way and you uncover a yellow jacket nest about the size of second base. And it's just covered with those ill-tempered little wasps. You hear a short "bzzzt" and a tip of fire begins to burn on the rim of your ear and that means you've been stung. Which means you may be stung twenty-five times. Therefore, fully clothed, you depart from the log and jump into the creek. At least that's what I did.

Misadventures of this sort give you the chance to judge your actions against those of others. Cousin C. T.'s, for example. That footlog event showed a basic difference between us.

C. T. would never abandon the log and splash into the creek just because he had been stung one time by a yellow jacket. He would wait until he'd been stung at least twice. Because he'd figure maybe the yellow jackets wouldn't send out any additional defenders and he could back off and reach the bank with dry pants and just one sting.

Not me. One sting was all I required. One sting and I would have leaped off the top of the windmill the same as I did off that log.

I admired C. T.'s capability to wait and see what happened but I came to believe he carried it too far, over into foolhardiness. You take snakes. If C. T. was crossing a footlog and came to a snake, he would stand there and visit with the thing a while until he determined what kind it was.

I understood why he did this and I approved of it as a reasonable course, for him. But not for me. As soon as I saw anything long and slithery on the log, I jumped into the creek.

"It ain't nothin' but a coach whip," he'd say after I'd jumped. I didn't care. Just being off the log and away from anything long and slithery was worth getting wet to me. It wasn't for C. T. When he saw snakes, he was able to remember that most of them are not venomous. I could remember that, too, but not until I was in the water.

He was that way about a lot of things. In summer

when we would sleep out in the yard, in the hot-weather custom of the country, I was always waking up and swatting at unseen creatures and leaping out of bed. Because if something with a lot of fuzzy legs came across my face in the night, I knew it was a black widow spider come to get me and I would jump four feet straight up.

C. T. would wait, I suppose to see if the creature would bite him. His position was that very few spiders are more poisonous than a chigger, so any one of them wasn't worth being excited about. But then you understand he was also the kid who would stand barefooted in the middle of a red ant bed and hold his breath and no ant would sting him.

To this day, if we were in the woods and decided to cross a new footlog, if he met a snake at the halfway point he would not jump off. However, I do think he would talk me into going across first.

The Chief Storyteller

Before he got old and sick and had those strokes, Uncle Billy Crockett was the chief storyteller in our clan. He is long dead now. Patted in the face with a shovel, as he put it, when he meant a person was gone and buried.

He was fond of that expression. "They'll pat me in the face with a shovel," he'd say, "before ever I'll vote anything but a straight ticket." Straight Democrat, that is.

Republicans were mighty scarce along the T&P in that Cross Timbers country where Uncle Billy lived out his time and told his stories.

I remember him talking about riding up to Kansas City or somewhere, maybe it was on into Nebraska, with a load of cattle. He was working then for one of those big ranches that would ship steers north, and somebody would ride along with them, all the way, to see they got water.

He'd ride on the caboose and sleep in it with the other cattle people who were along on the trip, and they'd cook beans and stew, and play cards. He was the only man I knew when I was growing up who had ridden on a caboose, and for that experience I held him in high respect. What a wonderful way to travel, as I imagined.

Sometimes we'd walk miles through the mesquite to the railroad and wait at a trestle for a freight and wave at the crew. The man in the caboose always looked so loose and important, slumped in his seat with an elbow on the window sill. He'd wave in slow motion. The style of the wave said he didn't mind doing it much, but he couldn't afford to show any enthusiasm. It was a gesture that meant, "So long, boys, I'm going all the way to Kansas City."

Uncle Billy Crockett, one of my personal kinfolks, had done that. Ridden a caboose and waved at boys. And he knew things about a caboose that we could tell at school.

Like how rough a ride it was. He would say: "You know when you're going into town with your daddy, and he trots the mules down that slope the other side of the Bosque, and those steel tires on the wheels get to bouncing on the rocks, how it feels when you're sitting in the wagon bed?"

Sure, we knew how that felt. It made your teeth rattle, and it blurred your eyes.

"Well," Uncle Billy would say, "that's about how rough a caboose is. I rode a saddle bronc one time in that Stamford rodeo that wasn't much rougher than a caboose."

In that way Uncle Billy educated us, broadened our horizons. But not always with accurate information. When finally, just a few years ago, I got a ride on a caboose, I thought of Uncle Billy when I climbed aboard and prepared myself for a shake-up. It was rougher than it looks, all right, but certainly not as rough as a steel-tired wagon bouncing down a rocky slope. Nothing on the planet is rougher than that.

What I started out to tell is about the Republican Uncle Billy met on that trip. He got creative about Republicans. We had never seen a Republican then, and Uncle Billy didn't mind testing us, to see how much we'd swallow.

"This one was a cattle buyer," he'd say. "He had lots of money. They're all rich, you know. Bills sticking out of pockets everywhere. They get their money from robbing honest folks like us."

We'd want to know what one looked like. How would we know one if he walked up off the road?

"You wouldn't, from a distance," Uncle Billy would say. "From a distance they look like ordinary humans. But you get up close to one, and you'll see there's a difference in the eyes. They're cold-eyed, kind of, and there's a thing they can do with their skin that normal folks like us can't do."

With their skin?

"You take one of your daddy's mules, that white one, Old Moon. He's standing out there in the horse lot, and a fly comes and lights on his shoulder, right about here. You know how he gets rid of that fly?"

We knew. He'd make his skin shimmy. Automatically, that little patch of Old Moon's hide where the fly sat would quiver and cause the fly to move. Which is a handy trick that all mules and horses can do.

"Well sir," Uncle Billy would say, and he'd lean forward and get right up in our faces, "a Republican can do that."

We'd laugh, knowing it couldn't be true. And yet isn't it interesting that the image, of a person's skin quivering that way, stays with me yet, half a century after Uncle Billy planted it.

Republicans in our country were so rare, I didn't even meet one until I went off to school. He was an economics prof. He didn't have cold eyes, though. I thought of telling him Uncle Billy's yarn about the fly and the mule. But I wasn't sure it would help my grade, and I was already weak in economics, so I let it go.

The day we finally patted Uncle Billy in the face with a shovel, he'd been sick a long time. A crowd of us stood around in that little Palo Pinto County cemetery to tell him so long. Something about us I'm glad he didn't know—that a solid majority of that bunch a few days before had voted for a Republican named Eisenhower. Uncle Billy wouldn't have understood that.

Don't Leave Him Talking

In his prime, Uncle Billy Crockett could hold any audience with his stories, but near the end of his time he lost most of his power.

Which didn't keep him from talking. He would often sit on the front porch and talk and talk and imagine that everybody was listening, when in fact nobody was paying him the slightest notice.

There was a gentle joke among the women who cared for Uncle Billy in this final chapter of his life. They were nieces, most of them. They loved him and kept him scrubbed pink and fed him soft meals that pleased his stomach and saw that he stayed warm.

The little joke was, "Don't go off and leave Uncle Billy talking."

On winter nights when we gathered in front of the fireplace and waited for bedtime, Uncle Billy would get on one of his talking spells, and if everybody walked out and left him he would just keep talking, talking into the fire until one of the women came and rescued him.

He didn't exactly tell stories, he simply talked, high and trembly. I would give a considerable sum now to have a recording of Uncle Billy's talking spells. Sometimes it pleases me to try to reconstruct one from what I remember hearing. This is the way he sounded:

"I was with that Faircloth bunch then, and some of the McCandless boys, too, and Grover Brady from down here at Huckaby. We went way over there on the Angelina and bought steers and commenced trailing them back west. I never saw such little bitty old pot-bellied cattle. One of those cow people we met said an East Texas steer could starve to death standing belly-deep in grass. That tall old grass, got no more kick to it than well water does.

"The second day out, here come a big rain and all the creeks flooded, and we lost ever one of those cattle trying to cross 'em over a little old branch. In that flood water they just swum away from us like ducks. I never knew cattle to swim that fast. What I figured, it was those pot bellies they had. Get one of them little cows in the water and wasn't anything to her but a big balloon with a head and tail and four legs, and the whole concern would just float off and leave you.

"Well, after we lost the cattle we set up camp on a kind of island in a creek bottom, to wait for the water to go down, and that oldest McCandless boy decided to make some whiskey. He'd brought biscuits in a syrup bucket and he took shelled corn his daddy carried for horse feed and boiled it in that bucket with his neckerchief spread over the top. Ever now and then he'd squeeze it out into a tin cup and finally he got enough to pass around and sip.

"It wasn't real whiskey because it was pure alcohol, and I sure didn't drink any. I didn't mind the alcohol, but I wouldn't want to drink anything that'd been squeezed out of Jim McCandless's bandana.

"Now you don't need to boil grain to get alcohol because alcohol is everywhere. That time I worked down on the Nueces, below Dog Town, they had what they called nockaway trees (I believe now he meant the anaqua tree) that put on sweet berries. One day I saw a big buck deer staggering through the brush, and they told me he'd got drunk eating nockaway berries.

"Well, I've known boar hogs to be drunk from ripe peaches. And mockingbirds? I've laid out yonder under the grape arbor and seen mockingbirds get so drunk on ripe grapes they couldn't sit on a bobwire fence.

"But you talk about fences, the best fence-builders I know are those Mexicans that do the rock walls down below the Rio Grande. They go out and gather up rocks by the ton and fit them all together in a wall two feet wide and six feet high and there's not a horse or a bull in Mexico or Texas could get across it. One of our bobwire fences ain't anything to a Mexican wall.

"But now your Mexican, he's a different proposition. When I was doing ranch work I made acquaintance out at Del Rio one time with a cow hand by the name of Manyull, and he showed me something about peppers. Now your peppers . . . "

Then one of the women would come, and pat him, and say, "Uncle Billy? Honey? Aren't you about ready for bed?"

A Liberated Stove

During a visit to my old hometown I was obliged to give a little talk at the library. One of my contemporaries came up after the meeting and grinned and said, "I notice you didn't mention the time we liberated the pot-bellied stove."

In the sense he used it, that verb "liberated" came out of World War II. I had not, of course, heard it yet at the time of the pot-bellied stove affair because that happened around 1936 or 1937 when we were country-town boys of about fifteen. We could have used a term like that to help us justify the act.

Four of us were fixing up a hand-made shack in the woods outside town, a place where we could hide out and smoke hand-rolled cigarettes and talk about girls. We decided we needed heat and ought to acquire a stove.

So we went to shop at Mr. Feldman's. The name might not have been Feldman, but it sounds right to me now. He operated what we would today call a flea market. We called it a junkyard then. Beneath a rickety shed behind Mr. Feldman's stood this fine little pot-bellied wood-burning stove, and all of us fell in love with the pretty thing and knew we had to have it. But buying it was impossible. There was not enough cash in that crowd to buy a soda pop. Every item of furnishing or equipment in the shack was brought from home or found in trash heaps.

So, seeing we had to have the stove, and there was no money to pay for it, one night we simply took it. We said we borrowed it. If we could have said we liberated it, that would have suited us better. Liberated a nice stove from a junkyard, where it had no business being.

When we got the stove cleaned and set up, we could see it was better than we thought. It looked too good, which bothered me. I suspected trouble would come from it, and I was right.

One day my father said he wanted to see the place where I'd been spending so much time. He didn't ask to see it. He said, "Come on, let's go."

In the shack he took a quick look around and locked onto the stove. He said, "That's a pretty nice-looking stove you boys have got here."

I told him yes sir, it's a nice stove all right.

"How'd you boys come by a stove like this?" he asked.

Told him I didn't remember exactly how we got that stove.

"Well, I bet if you thought about it a minute you could remember," he said, "because this stove is the best thing in the place. I don't believe you'd forget for very long how you got it."

He let me sit and hurt for a while. My father had this poisonous system for punishing sins. He'd make you suffer while you were confessing. He'd draw the confession out of you an inch at a time, and every inch a pain, so that finally you wanted to shout the truth at him so the ordeal would be finished and you could quit suffering. Time he got through with you you didn't need any additional punishment.

"Did you buy the stove?" he asked.

No sir, didn't buy it.

"Did somebody give it to you?"

Well, no sir, not exactly.

"Can you remember where it came from now?"

Told him I thought it came from Mr. Feldman's.

"Ah, Mr. Feldman's," my father said. "Did Mr. Feldman let you have it?"

Well, in a way he did. He didn't say we *couldn't* have it. It's a sort of borrowed stove, you might say.

"But Mr. Feldman doesn't know it?"

Yes sir, that's about it.

"If you borrow a thing without permission, what's that mean?"

Well sir, it means you took it, I guess.

"And if you *take* a thing that belongs to somebody else, what does that mean?"

He had me. I was tired holding out so I went ahead and said it meant stealing.

He helped me unhook the stove, and we returned it to Mr. Feldman's. I was needing somebody to share the guilt, and I told my father I wasn't the only one mixed up in taking the stove.

"Never mind that," he said. "You were mixed up in it, and that's all I'm interested in."

So I had to stand in front of Mr. Feldman and make the confession and take the rap for the entire stove, instead of just the one-quarter of it that was mine. My father monitored in a sinister silence, making sure I said everything right. It was a torture, and when I was back there not long ago where it happened, I could feel the pain again.

I told my partner in crime, the one who dug up the memory, something he didn't know: The irony of that caper was, when I returned the liberated stove, Mr. Feldman said he didn't know it had been gone.

Swinging in Church

A friend just called and invited me to go to church Sunday. He said it would do me good. I expect that's true, and I may go.

This gent said he bet I hadn't been inside a church for five years. No, I was in one just a month ago, over in Mississippi, and within the past two years I have been in churches at Nacogdoches, Bellville, San Antonio, and Rockport, and for a while in the Big Thicket I was under a brush arbor where a revival was being held.

If you count from long ago when I was in overalls and two-dollar tennis shoes, I have probably been in church as many hours as most preachers' kids. My Methodist mother looked for reasons to go to church, and take me with her.

I knew that church better than I knew the house we lived in. I could tell you how many seats were in the choir loft, and how many pipes the organ had. I knew the number of links in the chains of the light fixtures that hung from the ceiling. I could tell you what page "The Old Rugged Cross" was on in the hymn book and I knew where they kept the grape juice used in communion services.

If I had wanted to make a little wager—which I didn't because it was a sin to bet, and especially in church—I could have won money. I could have bet a dime on which old dude in the choir would go to sleep first, when the sermon began. I knew which ones to bet on. They were men who ran stores and worked fourteen hours a day six days a week. How were they going to stay awake sitting in the choir on Sunday?

My mother's message about going to church was, you went to learn how to be saved, so you wouldn't go to hell when you died. All right, I could see the sense in that.

But after I'd heard all the rules a hundred times, and had joined up, I got tired of listening and stopped. I'm not saying that was the right thing to do. I'm only saying that's what I did.

So I had all that church time to put in, and I looked for ways to make it pass. That's when I began counting choir seats, and pews, and links in chains and things like that.

Those light fixture chains had possibilities, hanging down about six feet from a high cathedral-type ceiling. There were six of them, three on each side of the center aisle, spaced something like twelve feet apart.

One Sunday when the sermon was along toward the

middle, I recognized that I could perform an astonishing stunt right there in church. I got the idea from *Tarzan of the Apes*, which was running as a serial on Saturdays at our picture show.

Tarzan was forever swinging through the jungle on grapevines, or whatever kind of vines they were, and I was able to see that I could do the same on those light fixture chains.

So I did it. I went up to the top of the balcony aisle, and got a running start, and pushed off the railing, and leaped out and caught the first chain on the right and swung on it a couple of times to get up momentum and then I let go and sailed over and caught on to the second chain. Do you see how I did it?

In that way, swinging from chain to chain as Tarzan did on his vines, I passed over the entire congregation, even directly over the head of the preacher, and it was a splendid trip. I can't think of anything I ever did that gave me greater satisfaction.

At the dinner table after church I thought of telling about my Tarzan feat on the chains, but nobody would have believed I really did it. So I have kept it to myself, all these years until now.

Sparrows and pigeons and wasps would fly into that church during services, and these were interesting events.

Before we got manufactured air, the tall stained-glass windows that churches have could actually be opened and shut. Among a church's equipment was a long wooden pole with a metal attachment at its end. This metal gizmo fit into corresponding hardware on the window frames and in that way the high windows could be opened or closed.

A very important person did this. I always supposed that in our church, nobody was more important than the man who got up during the sermon, and fetched the pole, and raised or lowered windows. He had to be a doctor, or a banker, or at least in the insurance business.

Well, I have got to run along but be sure to remind me to tell you about the time the pigeon flew into the church during the sermon, and flapped about among the light fixtures, and what the choir did when the pigeon perched on the organ pipes, and what the preacher said.

Brother Foster's Prayer

Did I ever tell you about Brother Foster's Thanksgiving prayer?

Long ago, out in that West Cross Timbers country beyond Fort Worth, Brother Foster was famous for prayers that showed scope and style. I once heard him send up a Thanksgiving prayer that was major league in all respects, and he did it standing in the kitchen door on Grandma Hale's farm.

This old fellow was not really a preacher. But in rural regions at the time I am talking about, purebred and registered preachers were scarce and people made do with the nearest they had to the real article.

Brother Foster taught Sunday school, and did funerals, and went around comforting the sick and sorrowful, and generally made a satisfactory substitute for a pastor. My father used to say you could put a black hat on Brother Foster and hand him a Bible and a collection plate and he could pass for a preacher at a Baptist convention.

There were whispered stories that Brother Foster would even do you a quiet and slightly invalid wedding, in case of an emergency where the need for quick nuptials was beginning to show. But I don't know if that was true, and even if it was, then I figure the old gent was simply rendering a public service, so let it go.

His specialty was prayers on special occasions, like at Fourth of July picnics, ice cream suppers, Christmas gatherings, and other holiday affairs. It must have been in '31 or '32 that Brother Foster came to Grandma Hale's farm for Thanksgiving dinner. All the women, especially, counted it a social triumph to have Brother Foster for Thanksgiving. I don't know how we got him, as he was spread pretty thin over that region.

The meal was the occasion for the prayer, so it was delivered as the blessing. Or asking the blessing, as we said, or returning thanks.

When the formal invitation was issued—"Brother Foster, will you return thanks for us?"—that luminary backed away from the table and took up a position in the doorway that led into Grandma's kitchen. Evidently he felt a need to be isolated from the general bunch.

He was a big, heavy-shouldered fellow with deep-set eyes and wavy white hair and a mighty voice. My father used to say that they ruined a first-rate preacher when they put Brother Foster to following a mule across a cotton patch.

He waited for silence before he began. If silence took a full minute to arrive, still he waited. We were supposed to keep our heads bowed and our eyes closed but by that time I had perfected a system of looking around at things through eyes that seemed closed but really weren't.

Brother Foster stood with his legs slightly apart and his hands behind him and his chin elevated and his eyes closed. Just when you thought he would begin, a foot would scuff or a throat would clear and he would hold off a while longer. Even a calf, bawling for its mama out at the barn, would delay his beginning.

He started out quietly, and built volume as he went

along. He began with the food and the blessed hands that prepared it. He called Grandma by name, and I learned later that this was a high blessing, to get your name sent up in a prayer by Brother Foster, and on Thanksgiving Day, at that.

From the women he went to the men who tilled the land and brought forth its fruits. He went on to thank the Lord for the beasts that pulled the plows, and those that sacrificed their lives to give us sustenance.

Then he took up the children and asked the Lord to bless their little hearts and keep them safe. (It didn't occur to me that he seemed to rank children behind mules and poultry, since this was before the age of child worship.)

He went into the field of medicine and thanked the Lord for protecting those of us who hadn't caught terrible diseases or suffered crippling injuries. He got into agriculture and mentioned the good corn crop, and the cotton crop which was fair. Went then to meteorology and pointed out to God that the rains came a little too late in the season but were appreciated anyhow. He called the names of people who had died during the year, people we knew, and he gave thanks for their lives. He gave thanks for breezes that turned windmills, for pretty music, for the love of friends and kinfolks, for the very roof over our heads, for feather mattresses on cold winter nights.

This litany went on until the dressing was cold and I thought it was more a sermon than a prayer. Not until a good many years later did I understand why Brother Foster's long prayers were sought and appreciated.

Life in that country was hard, and those folks needed somebody to remind them that they had a lot to be thankful for.

Grandma's Gas Well

Did I ever mention to you that I'm an oil heir? Well, I am, and to prove it I've got right here in my greedy hand a check for $18.65.

I get such a check every month and I don't have to do one foreign thing in return for it except sign my name on the back and put it in the bank. Of all the things I have done in this life to make a living, being an oil heir is the easiest. I sure like it.

Furthermore, some months the amount exceeds $18.65. Sometimes the check is $22.17. Other times, it's less than the price of a secondhand shirt, like maybe $7.00.

Would you like to hear how a person gets to be an oil heir?

In my case, all I had to do was be kin to Miley Ann Dickerson Hale. She was my father's mother and therefore my grandmother and that's why I get the check. The money comes out of a hole in the ground on Grandma Hale's farm in Erath County. About an hour's drive southwest of Fort Worth.

The oil people set up this rig north of the barn. I know the spot well. I once jammed a mesquite thorn in my foot at that well site. I remember how it felt, and how it took about a month of limping before the soreness went away.

I remember when the leases were being signed, we joked about it. It was a laughable idea that this somewhat pitiless place behind the barn on Grandma Hale's farm would produce anything worth a dollar.

But it did. I was just astonished. They made a well there. A gas well, really, not oil. If any oil is coming out of that hole my palms have not been greased with it. But I don't care to be called a gas heir. I like the sound of oil better.

I suppose you can tell by the size of my check that I am not having any trouble spending all my oil money. This is because there are two kinds of oil heirs and I am the second kind. Too bad.

The first kind doesn't have many kinfolks. So if the oil people come and make a well on their grandmother's old farm, they won't have to split the take with a raft of kin. This is the best kind of oil heir to be.

The reason my check is so small may be traced to the productivity of Grandpa and Grandma Hale. They had nine children and they were Bible readers who took seriously the part where the Lord said, "Go forth, and populate the earth." Did they ever populate it. They are one of the reasons baby doctors are now driving around in Porsches and BMWs.

When I heard the oil folks had made a well behind Grandma's barn, I got a numbers guy to explain to me what my interest in all those riches would be. He took a pencil and a piece of paper and spoke as follows:

"First you make yourself a decimal point, see, like this. Be sure you put it way over to the lefthand side of the page. Next you start drawing zeros, all in a row to the right of the decimal point. You keep making zeros until you run out of paper and then you pick a number and write it in. Any number you like. It won't make any difference by then. Say seven. Seven's a nice number. So you write a seven and stand back and count the zeros and that's about what your interest in this production is."

Which I thought was not a very nice way to talk about Grandma Hale's Gas Well, which we are all very proud of, despite that we are represented in the enterprise mainly by a string of zeros.

I study this little check for $18.65 and I make a wish. I

wish there was a magic way I could have handed $18.65 to the tired-eyed adults who were trying to dig a living out of that old farm in the 1930s. Grandma Hale was gone by then but the land was still in the family. In the Great Depression my own parents retreated to that farm one year, when they could no longer pay rent in town. That old place fed us. Its corn and its black-eyed peas and its milk and butter and eggs fed us, when we couldn't buy groceries at the store.

I think of what $18.65 would have done then for those struggling folks. That much cash, when a dollar was big as the moon? It might have made the difference between losing the farm and keeping it.

I told that numbers man that this must be a pretty good gas well. Because if I am getting $18.65 a month, with all my zeros, somebody up there close to that decimal point has got to be doing all right. He agreed.

That makes me remember things about the spot where the well is. In my recollection of the time we were all on the farm together, fighting for survival, that place beyond the barn has represented the worst of the scene. It was a poor part of the pasture. It seemed forsaken. Very little grass. Sharp rocks to hurt the feet. Mesquite thorns on fallen twigs. Horned frogs. Red ant beds. Goathead stickers. Lizards hurrying across, looking for shade.

When things died, they were taken to that place to be disposed of in nature's way, and buzzards were often there, either busy or waiting, and so it was not a part of the farm anyone went to by choice.

To me it's become one of the ironies of this life that only a few thousand feet below that ugly crust, a fortune was lying. We were picking our way over it, barefoot, to miss the goatheads and thorns and red ants. We were stepping over all that natural gas down there. The smallest part of it, no matter how far the zeros traveled from the decimal point, could have made us rich instead of poor.

VI

A LIFETIME
OF CHANGE

Pretty Nice Pay

There was a little Associated Press story out of New York a day or two ago about how much money Jim Manzi made in 1987. Manzi is the chairman of Lotus Development Corporation. He is thirty-six years old. The story said he made $26.3 million last year.

What I figured was that the decimal point had fallen into the wrong place and that the figure ought to be $2.63 million. Because $2.63 million seems a nice comfortable pay for the chairman of a corporation, enough at least to get him by.

But evidently $26.3 million is correct. The story also

---

said that Lee Iacocca made $17.9 million working for Chrysler and came in second to Manzi among corporate officers in the nation.

In 1986 Iacocca ran first. I wonder if he is feeling like a failure, making so much less than a guy of only thirty-six.

The story gave *Business Week* magazine as the source of those numbers. Manzi is not really on the payroll to receive $2 million per month. A lot of that money came from bonuses and stock options.

But doesn't it make your fingers sort of tingle to know that a person can have a job that pays them $26 million in one year? Why, that's more money than professional basketball players get for pitching a ball through a hoop.

I suppose we have to remember that these are inflated dollars we're talking about, and a million bucks just isn't what it once was. For instance, $26 million might not make a down payment on one of those B-2 bombers the Air Force is building—at $275 million per copy.

I wonder if Jim Manzi and Lee Iacocca are required to talk about their pay at home, the way my kinfolks in Palo Pinto County used to do long ago.

When one of the family grew up and left the farm and got a job in town, he was expected to tell how much he was earning. If he didn't volunteer to tell it, you can bet somebody would ask him.

The asker would be an elder in the clan, somebody like Uncle Billy Crocket whose seniority entitled him to ask anything of anybody, or so he thought.

One of his nephews, say, has gone into town and found a job and now has come home to visit and it's Sunday afternoon and everybody's sitting around on the porch and Uncle Billy says to the nephew: "Well, Tommy, what kinda work you doin' in Mineral Wells?"

Tommy says he's a carpenter's helper, that he fetches lumber and tools and nails.

"A carpenter's helper," Uncle Billy says. "What do they pay for work like that?"

Tommy says he started out at two bits an hour but he's getting thirty cents now, and putting in about ten hours most days.

You understand this is going on before an audience of maybe thirty-five or forty members of the family and everyone is now leaning forward, listening hard, and multiplying thirty times ten to see how much this young fellow is getting per day.

Uncle Billy says to Tommy, "So you're drawin' three dollars a day, for carryin' boards?"

Tommy says some days he puts in twelve hours and draws better than $3.50. This gets oh's and ah's from the audience.

Which encourages Tommy to state that in six months, when he learns more, the fellow he's working for has promised to put him on as a carpenter and he'll be drawing fifty cents an hour, maybe more. More oh's and ah's, louder.

Then Uncle Billy hits Tommy with the bad news, concerning Tommy's cousin Hubert: "Hubert's workin' at the feed mill in Weatherford and drawin' $125 a month and a Christmas bonus."

That information gets gasps and whistles from the crowd on the porch, and it's mighty deflating to Tommy because his cousin Hubert is a year younger.

I wonder if Lee Iacocca felt like Tommy, when he found out a youngster like Jim Manzi made $8.4 million more than he did, and now *Business Week* and Associated Press and hundreds of newspapers are spreading the story all over the country.

In our clan, spreading stories about the incomes of family members is a custom that probably hasn't died quite yet. I must have been fifty years old by the time I stopped hearing questions like, "What kinda work you doin' down there in Houston?" and "What do they pay for work like that?"

I always had a deep hankering to answer that last question with some outrageous number that would shock the overalls off them all.

Hey, I wonder if Jim Manzi would like to come down here for a visit. I could take him to the country and find folks who still ask such questions.

They would say to him, "What kinda work you do up there in New York?"

He would say he is the chairman of a large corporation and then they would ask, "What do they pay for work like that?"

He could answer sort of casually, and say, "Well, last year I made $26.3 million." It would be interesting to watch the faces react to that news.

◆──────────────────────────────◆

Summers of Softball

When I take a walk in the park I stop sometimes and watch an inning or two of a softball game. I lean against the fence and listen to the chatter of the infielders and I think about the summer of '36 back in my old hometown.

That was when organized softball came to our community and made it a better place. The volunteer firemen built a lighted field down by the depot and men and boys from all over town were organized into teams. We played a schedule that lasted three months. Nobody had any money to go on vacation and so for several years, softball was our principal summer activity.

We would have tournaments and teams from other towns would come to play. The stands would be packed with spectators and cars full of people would be parked all the way down the foul lines on both sides.

The reason for the popularity of softball was that players of all ages took part. A boy of sixteen might play on the same team with the principal of the high school. Or he might bat against his doctor. Or catch a fly ball hit by the chief of police. In the batting order he might hit just ahead of the mailman, or he might follow the manager of the department store.

So those summer softball games were a way for young guys to get acquainted with the older men and it was a good thing for our town. A boy could walk into the bank on Saturday morning and the teller would know that he was the one who caught the fly in deep center field for the third out in the last inning on Friday night.

This was when flashy-colored uniforms began to be the fashion, instead of the traditional dull gray of baseball suits. About six o'clock you would see men and boys from every part of town, walking to the ball park in their uniforms. They liked to walk, so they could be seen.

I remember a fellow, a sort of farmer type, who was about thirty-five years old. He told us one night that the only reason he had joined a team was that he wanted to wear one of those uniforms. He had gone out for football and basketball in high school but he wasn't good enough to win a suit.

That's what we called it then, winning a suit. It was an honor to have a uniform, even if you didn't get to play much.

I think about that now when I walk by a playground where little children who look like they're in the first grade are out there running around in pretty new uniforms and fancy athletic shoes. They look very cute and colorful but those youngsters will never understand the honor of winning a suit, the way that farmer did. They won't be able to remember when they *didn't* have a suit.

I don't believe the men and boys of our town ever got along better than they did those summers when we were all playing ball together.

There was a lawyer in our town and I sometimes did some yard work for him, mowing and clipping and weeding flower beds. He was mighty particular and acted cranky when I didn't do the work exactly as he wanted it done. Tell you the truth, I didn't much like him.

One night he showed up on my team. Somebody had quit and we needed an outfielder and that lawyer volunteered. So suddenly instead of being my boss he was my teammate, dressed exactly the way I was. And instead of fussing at me for not edging the flower beds right, he was rooting for me, and I for him. He turned out to be a pretty good fellow, and he had a fair arm, too, although he wasn't so much with a bat.

I remember two preachers who played. My own preacher was one. He always struck me as being solemn and dignified and deliberate in church. But put a uniform on him and he became a thief and a con man. On the base paths he was a jackrabbit.

He would steal a base and slide in and cut a guy's feet flat out from under him. And sneaky? That minister was sure full of tricks. He had a fake throw that would have fooled angels.

On Sunday I would study him in the pulpit. He'd be reading scripture and saying prayers and being so religious. I couldn't believe he was the same dude who beat us the night before with a little old dinky drag bunt in the seventh inning.

We had another gent who was a big man with the Boy Scouts, and was often pointed out as setting a good example for youth. Softball gave him a hard time because he was a weak hitter. He wanted to knock the ball over the railroad tracks every time he came to bat, I suppose so he could be a hero for the Boy Scouts in the stands.

But the harder he swung, the farther he missed, and the more he fanned, the madder he got. I have seen him duck behind the stands, out of sight, and bang his bat into the dirt and make low, muttery noises that sounded a lot like cussing to me.

What I learned from those summers of softball was that we were all so much alike. I was surprised by that. I hadn't imagined that a preacher or a lawyer or a banker or a scoutmaster could ever have anything in common with me.

But they did, when it came to playing that summer game under the lights down by the depot. When we got the uniforms on, we all wanted to do the same thing—get up there and blast one half across the county, and win, and get talked about the next morning on the courthouse square.

Country Weeklies

Back when I was doing more traveling than I do now, the first place I'd go when I drove into a small town would be the newspaper office. We had lots of good old country weekly papers in Texas then, and I loved to hang around them. I learned a great deal from country editors.

I am talking about just after World War II. We still have many small-town newspapers, but they are not old-style country weeklies. The present ones may be better papers, I don't know, but they don't have the character of the Texas weeklies I loved in the late forties up through the sixties.

You go into a country newspaper now and you might as well be walking into an insurance office for all the character you'll find. You can't even smell any ink. Very likely the paper's not printed in its own town, but in a big offset plant somewhere else. One way you can tell is that the people in the office have white hands. Haven't even got any ink on their fingers.

And some small-town papers now have secretaries, for crying out loud in church. Actual secretaries, young and smiling in pretty clean dresses. Sitting there answering the phone.

I am all in favor of secretaries but I can't get used to seeing them in country newspaper offices. At the kind of paper I'm talking about, you'd go in and find the editor, publisher, proofreader, printer, pressman, and advertising manager—and they would all be the same man. Actually you might not find anybody at all in the office. It wouldn't be locked up, but there'd be nobody there because the editor was going around the courthouse square, hustling ads.

Or if he was in the office he might be setting type or locking up a page and feeding a flatbed press.

I always enjoyed watching a country editor operate a Linotype machine. Lots of the old country editors had printers in the back shop to set type, but some could set it themselves. I used to stand behind Archer Fullingim and watch him write one of those long looping Page One columns he did for the *Kountze News.* He composed it on the Linotype. That takes confidence, not only in the ability to produce a good sentence but also to operate the machine. It's kin, at least, to carving words in stone, since the words were cast directly into metal type.

Long ago when I was going to school I had an itch to be a country newspaper editor. I scratched the itch a time or two, and it went away. But I had it to begin with because I never could see myself working for a big-city daily. I didn't figure I would fit, and the idea of being a country editor appealed to me. I had read stories about country editors and they led wonderful lazy lives.

They didn't work but about three days a week, according to the stories. They just sat around, and people brought them the news, and they printed it on Thursdays and went fishing until about Tuesday of the next week. That sounded all right to me.

Then I began getting acquainted with a few country editors and their lives weren't exactly the same as the stories had said. A few of them managed to stay lazy, true, but those had a habit of going broke or living right on the verge of bankruptcy. I noticed the ones who made a good living seemed to work awful hard. That made me nervous about the country weekly business, and I decided to keep away from it.

Big-city newspapermen used to sit at bars a lot after they got off work and talk about leaving town and going where the pace was slow to start a country newspaper. They'd dream of living long relaxed lives as country editors.

A few of them I've known actually left, too, and some came back. A couple who didn't come back are John and Marie Moore, friends of mine who used to work for the dailies here in Houston. They took off and went down to Friendswood. Started a little paper.

For about ten years they worked as hard as anybody I ever watched. I'd go down there to see them living that slow life, and they were always working, every day, and most nights as well. I got worried about them.

They ended up with two or three papers and finally sold out, and now when I see them they seem to grin a lot and I expect they've done mighty well. But they didn't do it on a three-day week, like I was figuring on when I wanted in the country newspaper business. They did it on about a ten-day week.

Across the years, once in a great while, I have seen something that made me itch again about the life of a country editor. For instance: One day I was walking across the Austin County square in Bellville, and the fire whistle blew. Presently here came the fire truck, roaring across the square. Its driver swung left, braked abruptly in front of the *Bellville Times*. Franz Zeiske, editor and publisher of the *Times*, came out the front door putting on his hat. He swung smoothly onto the back of the truck, which then roared off to the fire, with Zeiske aboard to cover the story.

I thought that was wonderful. Nothing to equal that, for prestige, has ever happened to me in the big-city newspaper business.

East Texas Old and New

Driving out of Lufkin on Texas Highway 103, toward Louisiana. Loafing along, thinking kind thoughts about the fellow who invented air conditioners for automobiles. Temperature at 11:00 a.m. must be close to 100, if you measured it on the surface of the asphalt.

And look yonder at that boy, maybe ten years old, hiking along the edge of the blacktop and he's barefooted as he was when he entered this world. Makes the bottom of my feet burn to see him stepping on that hot pavement.

He'll be putting on his shoes pretty soon. The signs are already here, telling us that fall is creeping up on East Texas. The color of the woods is no longer bright, fresh green. It's more like olive drab now.

You can look into a thicket and see sunlight back in there, maybe 200 yards deep, when a month ago you'd have seen nothing but solid green. Foliage on the hardwoods is getting tired, drying out, beginning to rustle. Won't be long before leaves start falling.

A few sycamores are already yellow and sending down foliage. It's one of my favorite indicators of fall in East Texas—a carpet of sycamore leaves covering the sandy front yard of a country house.

You see other signs. People splitting fireplace wood. Letting the goat weeds and the crabgrass have what's left of the garden. Buying notebooks and pencils in the stores.

The weather and the seasons may be the only things about East Texas that haven't changed since I came to this part of the state in 1946. East Texas was still Old South then. For a guy in my business it was a wonderful place to work. To hear stories told with drawls and grins. To hang around country stores. To sit on front porches and creek banks and visit with the folks and let your heart beat slow, in time with theirs.

A lot of that kind of thing is still with us in East Texas but it doesn't *look* like that sort of place any longer. I have to search now to find what I think of as the old East Texas, which I loved. I loved it for selfish reasons, I admit.

The new East Texas is very likely a better place to live. More progress, more opportunity, all that stuff. I don't like it as well but that's not important to anybody but me. The bankers and the real estate people and the merchants like it better and that's what counts.

Sometimes I get lonesome for the old East Texas and I go in this direction, toward the Louisiana border. I like to start at Milam, in Sabine County where Highway 103 intersects Highway 87. Then go south, through Hemphill, Yellowpine, Burkeville, Newton, until I get enough.

I used to drive that road when you had to watch out, especially at night, because you might come around a curve and half a dozen cows would be bedded down in the middle of the blacktop. Highway 87 has changed a lot because of Toledo Bend Reservoir, which brought in so many new people with money to spend. But it's still old East Texas to me.

I like to stop a while on the courthouse square at Hemphill. That's the most old East Texas town in the Piney Woods, to my notion, the Sabine County courthouse square. Every time I return, it looks more artificial, more like a movie set. Yet nothing in this state was ever more real, more nearly honest.

Explaining why the square in Hemphill is old East Texas is not easy for me. It involves scale, and arrangement. The narrowness of the streets and the closeness of the buildings. And the way the storefronts look almost exactly how East Texas stores looked half a century ago.

Then you have the old county jail jammed right up against the courthouse, at the center of town, as if its presence there is reminding everybody, "You keep straight, or here's where you'll get put."

And on the courthouse square corner, beneath the great cedar tree and across the street from Western Auto and J. B. White's, they still have the domino tables for the men. They'll be there playing, no matter if the temperatures goes to 104.

Some of old East Texas is even more vague, hard to define for me. In Hemphill it has to do with the display of merchandise on the loading dock in front of Fuller's Feed Store, half a block off the square. Wheelbarrows, bushel baskets, saddles, two-gallon buckets, cartons of mason jars, rural mailboxes—something about that says old East Texas.

How about new East Texas? To me, new East Texas is a lake. Surrounded by resort developments, fish camps, trailer houses, bass boats, beer joints, and real estate signs.

A traveler seldom sees old East Texas towns now because they're hidden by commercial development out on the highways. Best example I've noticed on this trip is Jasper.

As a traveler, I now see Jasper consisting of one intersection, where Highways 96 and 190 cross. And here's what Jasper has: Exxon. Texaco. Gulf. Burger King. McDonalds. Sonic. Wal-Mart. Pizza Inn. Pizza Hut. Kentucky Fried. Pay & Pack. Eckerd's. Payless. Beall's. Ramada Inn.

That part of Jasper is clean and new and covered over with asphalt but it doesn't look like East Texas. It looks like a suburb of Dallas. It strikes me that a lot of East Texas towns are now looking like Dallas suburbs and I suppose they are happy to be that way. I hope so.

Hey, I notice the leaves on the black gum trees are already turning red and purple, reminding us that another autumn is going to come, after all. See you on down the road.

Mono Line and Store-Bought Bait

At La Grange I stopped to get gas a couple of blocks west of the courthouse square and I had a few minutes to watch two young boys, walking along the highway toward the Colorado River. Going fishing.

They look about eleven to me, maybe twelve, and this was the first time they'd gone fishing since school turned out for the summer. I could tell by the way they walked, with quick steps and eagerness, wanting to be there now, not ten minutes later but right now.

For a few seconds I was able to feel what those youngsters felt. A sort of anxiety, part pleasant and part uncomfortable. A feeling that says, "Something good is about to happen but I'm not sure I can wait." We used to feel it on the way to going swimming. Or waiting for the soda skeet to draw us big frosty mugs of root beer. Or walking to the picture show on Saturday afternoons.

Later on this coming summer when they go to the river again, and again, those boys won't be stepping so fast because some of the eagerness will have worn off by then.

I watched them grow smaller while they hurried along

and I wondered, "Could they be me, and a friend, half a century ago?" We always walked to the river in that same quick way just after school turned out.

No, it couldn't be me or any of my contemporaries in that scene and I'll tell you why.

First place, both those boys carried rods and reels loaded with monofilament line, and one had a little shallow tackle box. The reels were the closed-face spin-cast things, the cheap kind you see wrapped in plastic and hanging on racks in hardware stores.

But to me, at the age these boys are now, such a rod and reel would have been a technological marvel. I'd have been carrying a cane pole, or maybe just a pocketknife for cutting a pole off a willow tree.

Another thing, these boys weren't barefooted. They wore sneakers, without socks. I don't see many barefoot kids any longer. I am acquainted with people sixteen years old who have never gone barefooted. Isn't that a shame? Think of the rich experience they have missed.

They'll never know the delight of stepping on grass burs and thorns and rusty nails and sharp-cornered rocks. They won't ever know the thrill of scorching their feet by tippy-toeing along a concrete sidewalk on the fifteenth day of August. They'll enter into adulthood without every having a stone bruise, or a stubbed toe. Or a *stumped* toe, as we called it.

Also, they don't wear overalls now. They wear jeans or shorts. And T-shirts, and some of the T-shirts are so long they reach down below the knees. If I had gone out in public in my youth wearing a T-shirt drooping as far as they droop now, the big boys would have whistled and called me Mildred and I would have been mortified.

Something else is that these kids weren't wearing straw hats, as we always did in summer. They wore gimmie caps, adjustable to fit most heads. The only young folks I see wearing straw hats now are the cowboys driving black pickups. Wide-bodied pickups that somehow can accommodate from four to six skinny behinds on one seat. With the hat brims overlapping.

Then the bait. The boys carried a plastic carton of worms, the kind you buy at bait houses. Or even at convenience stores. I would like to think that they dug worms out of a cow lot and just happened to find a plastic carton to put them in. But I know better.

One detail of that scene happened to fit the way it would have been fifty or sixty years ago. A dog was with those boys, and he looked exactly right.

He was of no particular breed. I can't even describe what color he was. He looked properly malnourished, the way all dogs looked long ago. Also he trotted crooked, with his hind legs seven or eight degrees off the course being followed by his front ones.

It somehow comforts me that mongrel dogs, at least, have not changed much from the time I went barefooted to rivers in spring. I can still predict dogs like that. Let me tell you what this one did, as soon as he got to the Colorado with those boys.

When they slipped up silently and picked a quiet pool where the perch would be biting, what that dog did was leap into the middle of it and paddle around for a while, until all the fish were alerted and had swum upstream a quarter of a mile.

The Consummate Toy

Driving along West Gray near where it crosses Montrose, I slowed down to watch three little boys playing catch. What got my attention was that they were using an orange for a ball.

I wonder if there is a country in the world where children don't play ball in one form or another. Don't you agree that the ball is the consummate toy? High technology has come to the design and production of playthings and yet, what most children still play with is a ball, one of the simplest toys of all. If they don't have a store-bought ball they'll find a substitute, as the boys there on West Gray did.

In my early times we played catch with what we called bodark balls. This was the fruit of the Osage orange tree, or the bois-d'arc. Also called hedge apple. The tree produces its seed in a big globe that looks like a green oversized orange. And when somebody throws one to you, you better get your mitts up because if it slips through your hands and hits you in the teeth you can call time out and go to the dentist.

In the country, store-bought baseballs would be worn out in a month and when they were beyond repair we would make do with natural objects. I have played hours and hours of catch with green apples and pears. These little round striped gourds made pretty good balls, too. There were hard as rocks but that was all right for playing catch. I seem to remember we sometimes played, in fact, with rocks.

Something is deep inside human creatures that makes us want to pitch objects to each other, and catch them, and throw them back. If we can't do it we need to watch others do it. These young fellows who become millionaires now playing ball, they are the ultimate beneficiaries of this odd human need to throw, and catch, and strike a rounded object.

Histories of the most ancient people are apt to show mention of ball games. The prophet Isaiah has a line in Chapter 22 of the book he wrote in the Bible: "He (the Lord) will surely violently turn and toss thee like a ball . . ." Which sounds to me a lot like a second baseman pivoting and throwing to first on a double play. But the Bible does show at least that Isaiah was familiar with playing ball and he was operating 800 years before Jesus Christ was born.

I have been in the country in circumstances when we were so fiercely motivated to play some kind of ball that we would manufacture a ball to play with. We'd tear up parts of an old wagon sheet, or a worn-out cotton sack, and wind strips of the material into a ball and tie it with twine and a dozen country kids would spend half a day playing with that handmade ball.

A few months ago I took a canoe trip on Buffalo Bayou, from Voss down to the West Loop, and saw that one of the ways that stream is polluted is with tennis balls. Green tennis balls, dozens of them, floating in the bayou. I thought about my early times when we would have thought it a windfall to find a tennis ball floating in a creek. It would surely have been fished out and played with.

We played a game with a tennis ball and a broomstick that's interesting to me now because it's similar to the stick-ball played on the streets of New York and other big cities in the East. Out on the T&P Railroad west of Fort Worth we had never heard of stickball, and in fact we had just barely heard of New York. Yet boys were playing almost the same game in the turn rows of West Texas cotton patches that was being played on the streets of Harlem.

We had big old long-legged country boys who were held in respect on the schoolyard because they could swing a broomstick and knock an old tennis ball across the creek. I wonder now where those tennis balls came from. There wouldn't be a tennis court within fifty miles of where those broomstick games were played, and some of those kids would reach voting age before they ever saw a tennis racket. But there always seemed to be tennis balls around.

Golf balls, too. When I discovered along with my contemporaries that there were such things as golf courses in the world, we would roam across them and pick up lost balls and sometimes we'd come home with a tow sack half full. That many golf balls made up a great treasure.

The girls would go through them and pick out two or three of the best ones to use for playing jacks. A golf ball is excellent for jacks if you've got a sidewalk to play on where it'll bounce well. Then we would take the bulk of the golf balls and invent games, games that hadn't anything whatever to do with golf.

Did you ever hit a golf ball with a baseball bat? Oh listen, that's really fun because you can send that ball hundreds of yards. You hit it fungo style, by pitching it up and swinging when it came down. Because nobody was fool enough to stand out in front of you and pitch to you. It would have been like standing in front of a 35 mm gun. But when you caught a golf ball out there on the fat part of the bat, it was a wonderful feeling. For that instant you were the most powerful swinger on the planet, and there was tremendous satisfaction in seeing that little ball flying, flying into nowhere.

Carrying Water Again

The supermarket in my neighborhood has got an extraordinary amount of shelf space devoted to bottled water. I am talking about water for drinking and making coffee and tea and ice cubes.

Having several feet of grocery shelf space set aside for bottled drinking water is something recent to me. I'm surprised by it. All these people carrying water home, instead of drinking what comes out of the faucets over the kitchen sink.

For me it means a full circle has turned. When I discovered America, water piped into the house was a treasured convenience and the families who enjoyed that luxury were counted to be privileged.

This state was then populated by millions of rural folks who were dipping their drinking water out of creeks. Or drawing it out of cisterns or wells. And many were still hauling their water in barrels from distant sources. When the women needed a gallon, they went to the barrel with a bucket and dipped in and carried it to the kitchen.

Now look what we've got. Women carrying water again. I see them sometimes at grocery stores, lugging plastic water jugs to their cars. This is strange to me.

When I was living among country kinfolks back in the thirties, out west of Fort Worth, we depended on three sources for water. The most common was the cistern.

In dictionaries a cistern is defined as a receptacle for holding liquid. Where I came from, a cistern could be two things. It could be a large metal tank, mounted on a sturdy wooden platform. Or it could be a hole in the ground like a well, which was the second source.

A cistern was fed by runoff from the roof of the house. Gutters along the eaves—just like we have now—collected the rain. But instead of dumping the rain in the flower beds the water ran into the cistern.

In dry times when a thunderstorm approached, we'd all gather on the porch to watch, just in case the clouds dropped enough rain to make water run off the roof into the cistern. We loved to see water going in there.

Here on the Upper Gulf Coast, which is usually a wet part of the state, most country families now have wells and not cisterns. A well means a hole has been dug down into water-bearing sands, and the water collects in the bottom and is brought up by an electric pump.

In my early times in West Texas I never saw a pumped water well. I know now they existed. The pumps were powered by gasoline motors. I just didn't know about them then.

To me a well meant salty water. I always preferred cistern water, even though it sometimes tasted like the cedar shingles on the roof.

The third source of water was the nearest stream.

Parents today would be appalled to see their children drinking from a stream of water running along behind the house. A multitude of citizens who drank that way are still alive. I count myself among that number.

Here's a scene familiar to me: Early in August. No rain. Grass gone. Ground dusty. Sky high and gray. Water in the cistern tasting bad. Might have something dead in it. Maybe a rat.

Uncle John hitches the mules to a sled. Yes, a sled, that slides across the sand and clay and rocks. Sled has heavy runners made of four-by-four timbers. A fifty-gallon wooden barrel rides on the sled.

He walks behind the mules. Two miles. Three, maybe.

Goes to a pool on the creek. Using a two-gallon bucket, he dips and pours until the barrel is full. Hazes the mules back home. Getting that barrel of water takes an entire day of work, not counting chores.

Anybody who wants a drink, they get it out of the barrel. That precious water is not wasted on frivolous things, like baths.

In September the rains came and filled the cistern and the stock tank. But until then, the barrel on the sled was the water system.

Children learned from that barrel.

They learned to look before they put the dipper in the barrel to get a drink because they didn't want to dip up a drowned grasshopper or a dead wasp.

When the level of water in the barrel got low, mosquito eggs had hatched and the water was alive with tiny larvae and a kid learned to drink carefully from a dipper and say, "I didn't swallow a single wiggle-tail."

Don't you suppose that would seem marvelous to the young homemakers carrying drinking water out of supermarkets now? If they had lived two or three generations ago, they'd be carrying the water in and telling their children, "Be careful now, and don't swallow any wiggle-tails."

Not to Be Trusted

One of my grandmothers, who was known to all the family as Grandma Hale, was opposed to electricity. She held that it was not to be trusted. She took the position that electricity was mysterious and unpredictable and a first cousin to lightning. The last page she read before she died was illuminated by a kerosene lamp, and so was the first.

Grandma glided through the Pearly Gates in 1927 but I'm still reminded almost daily of her problem with electricity. I'm afraid I inherited a part of it.

I supposed in the beginning that she simply had an aversion to a modern convenience, and refused to accept change. But since 1939, twelve years after Grandma died, I have shared her mistrust of everything electric.

Maybe I shouldn't admit this, because it wouldn't be much of an exaggeration to say that I am enslaved by electricity. Served by it, yes, but almost totally dependent on it for my pay, my food, the comfort of my shelter.

The computer I'm typing on right now is plugged into an electrical circuit. The light I work by is powered off the same circuit. Yonder in the kitchen, the pot of soup simmering for my lunch is on an electric stove. Electricity spins the squirrel-cage fan that pushes conditioned air into the apartment.

When I feed this report to the *Chronicle* downtown, so I can get paid for what I do, it goes by telephone, which won't work without electricity. The Great Computer that lives beneath Texas Avenue, and which receives and consumes what I send in, would stop pulsing and growling and die without electricity. It *lives* on electricity.

If all electric power suddenly shut down, I would go out and sit on the curb and wonder what to do. And yet I am still afraid of the stuff.

The reason I remember 1939 as the year this began, I was getting ready to go to my high school graduation ceremony. I was putting mineral oil on my hair, so it would be properly greasy and shiny. Brillantine was better than mineral oil because it was spiked with sweet-smelling stuff. But it was way too expensive. You could buy a quart of mineral oil for what you'd pay to get five ounces of Brillantine.

Anyway, while I was lubricating my head with mineral oil, the bathroom light went out. It was a light that hung by a cord from the ceiling. The cord had a socket at its end. The bulb dangled just above the head of the person standing at the bathroom mirror.

In those times, when a light bulb quit shining you didn't assume that it was burned out. You fiddled with it, and hoped that it would shine again. People didn't have supplies of replacement bulbs in their closets the way they do now. If a bulb burned out, you stole one from a bedroom lamp or else you went forth and bought a new one. You bought bulbs one at a time, not in cartons. This is the way things were.

So on that important night in 1939 I reached up and fiddled with the bathroom light bulb and it exploded. This was an important event to me. The bits of glass that flew away from that explosion didn't really do me any physical harm. But they did me a lot of another kind of harm.

To this day, I am unable to screw a bulb into a socket without the expectation that it's going to explode in my face and put my eyes out. It has never happened again, not in forty-eight years. That doesn't matter. I still think it might.

When that bulb blew up, I could hear Grandma Hale saying, "See? I told you."

Other events have supported her stance on electricity. A major one is, say I'm in a motel in Lufkin or down in Victoria and I move a lamp, so I can have light to work. And when I push the plug into the outlet, something spectacular happens. There's a frying pop, and fire shoots forth, and black stuff appears on the wall around the outlet, and afterward the TV won't work.

I hate that because I'll need weeks, months, to get over the feeling that I can't push a plug into an outlet without expecting an explosion.

It's not reasonable to imagine I could get along without it but I do think Grandma Hale was right—you had better not turn your back on electricity because it's not to be trusted. It's mysterious and unpredictable and the first cousin to lightning.

The End of the World

Maybe you read in the paper, as I did, that the world is coming to an end.

This news came out of Raleigh, North Carolina, in an Associated Press story. It quoted from a book called *88 Reasons Why the Rapture Will Be in 1988* by Edgar C. Whisenant.

I haven't read the book yet, but I will because I've always had an interest in the end of the world, and how it's going to happen, and especially *when* it will happen.

Judging from the AP story, Whisenant's book says the end of the world is just now beginning and that it will take several years before the process is complete. November of 1995 seems to be the nearest Whisenant comes to giving a date. Mark your calendar.

I can't remember how many end-of-the-world predictions I have survived. At least two dozen, I bet. I do remember the first one, which came and went in 1933. The best one was four years later. I look on it as the best because I was privileged to take part in its observance, back in my old hometown.

In those times, when so many folks were out of work and the living was hard, every year we had at least one serious prediction about the end of the world. By serious prediction, I don't mean the seriousness with which the prediction was made. I mean instead the seriousness with which it was taken. There were standards.

The first requirement was that the person doing the predicting had to be a long way off. He couldn't be as close to us as Fort Worth, or even Corpus Christi. We wanted him at least in Arkansas. Arkansas was a good state then for such things, because it has mountains.

We wanted mountains. Say a person had somehow figured exactly when the world would end. What he did was gather his family and his followers together and get up on the highest hill he could climb and there he waited, issuing statements daily.

The thing was, we didn't have any confidence in local predictions. If a person we knew, there in town, had shouted from the steps of the courthouse that the world was shutting down next Tuesday, we'd have laughed him out of the county.

What made the 1937 prediction so popular was that it came off a mountainside in Colorado. That was better than Arkansas. We'd not had a prediction out of the Rockies, or anywhere that far west.

Furthermore, the guy making the prediction had quit his job and gone into the wilderness to wait for the end. That was not a detail. It was a major factor. Jobs then were so treasured, we couldn't conceive that a man would walk away from one if he didn't know the end was near.

Also, he had a firm date. It wasn't months or years in the future. It was Saturday afternoon at four o'clock.

The bunch I was running with then in the old home-town was mighty interested in that prediction. Did we truly believe the end would come?

No. And yet, we didn't discount it entirely. We joked about it, just as I am doing right here, but when that Saturday approached, the jokes got a little hollow.

We'd gather on the corner by the drugstore and talk about the way the end would be, how it would feel, what we'd see.

Some said there'd be a great earthquake, and an explosion, and everything would be pulverized, and afterward there'd be nothing. Just silence, and dust settling. Dust? Settling on what?

Others grinned and said no, there'd be a flood, and the water would rise and rise, and houses and windmills and barns and even the bank would be sucked down into mighty whirlpools and never seen again. Seen? Seen by whom? Wouldn't even be a grasshopper left.

It's of interest to me now that those long-ago end-of-the-world predictions didn't follow the Bible version. Most were big-bang theories—that the end of world would come in a terrible instant.

I remember the nervous gags we made. Hey, world's coming to an end Saturday so I don't have to study for the algebra test. Things like that.

Then we'd giggle and talk about where we'd go on Saturday, when the Time came. Some said on top of the courthouse, be a good place. Some said up on the hill on the west side of town. Notice we picked high places. The mountain syndrome. Nobody wanted to be in a low place. Nearer to heaven, I guess. Farther from hell?

When four o'clock Saturday came and nothing happened, we went out and played ball, or dug worms to go fishing, and pretended we never really gave the prediction a serious thought.

Why the Yard Was Swept

There were parties in those days. They were held at un-painted country houses with clean-swept yards. This was long ago when one of my jobs, getting ready for the great event, would be to clean the yard so it would be fit for company to walk on.

The yard was fenced with chicken wire and wobbly posts to keep out the cows and the horses. When party preparations began, creatures on the farm would come up to the fence and watch in wonder. Rhode Island Red hens that scratched for a living in the pastures would stand at the gate and make nervous clucks. Turkeys would stretch their necks and swivel their heads and try to see why the rhythm of the farm had changed. Something was happening, something different.

The dogs, too, were puzzled by the activity. People were taking baths in the middle of the afternoon. Women were scrubbing the porch with sudsy water left over from the baths and saying things like, "Law, we'll *never* get ready in time." Girls were sitting in the sun drying their hair and talking about who might come to the party and who might not and their voices were pitched high and the words came fast and they all looked down toward the mail-box, as if somebody might arrive four hours early.

This change of tone and pace was a curiosity to the dogs and they sat with ears erect and tails wiggling, not certain whether they ought to be happy or worried. The mules out in the lot stood at attention, their heads above the split-rail fence, eyes glued on the house and the yard. All the animals were a little nervous and confused. Here were cows being milked two hours early, and pigs fed long before sundown. Even the cats could tell something special was up, and they slunk low to the ground and kept their heads turning and their eyes watching for threats. Most were young and no parties had been held yet in their time.

Men were laughing and making jokes about the foolishness of parties, but they came in early from the field and took their baths and shaved with straight razors and put on church clothes.

Yards in the country at the time I am talking about seldom had grass. More likely a yard would be hard-packed dirt and it could get dirty the way a floor did and so it needed to be swept and picked up. We gathered mesquite thorns and dead leaves and rusty staples that had popped out of the fence. We picked up sticks and clods and pebbles and we swept the yard over and over until it was slick as slate and if a dog threatened to trot across it we would swing a broom at him because we didn't want any tracks showing.

When we got the yard ready we sat on the door of the storm cellar and talked about the smells coming out of the kitchen. Popcorn being popped. Candy being made. Chicken being fried, on Saturday afternoon instead of Sunday. How strange that was, and good.

The best time for one of these parties was a cool calm night, the kind that promised frost before morning. Kerosene lanterns would be hung out on the porch and everybody looked better in the dim light.

Lanterns at country parties always upgraded personal appearance. Girls, for instance. The homely ones looked nice. The plain ones looked pretty. The pretty ones looked beautiful. These were exciting times.

The men and boys had a curious appearance at parties. It had to do mainly with hair, which would be pasted down with water and combed slick and then patches of it would dry out here and there and start poking up and this gave a sort of spikey effect, similar to these punk haircuts you see nowadays.

There would be games. Simple games that made the heart pound. Names would be drawn out of a hat, a girl's name and a boy's, and the two would then hold hands and walk all the way around the house in the dark and the boy would have to make clever remarks to entertain the girl during the trip. I would say, "I swept the yard." And she would say, "You did?" Just as if sweeping yards was a noble calling and nobody without creative talent could sweep one.

We'd have songs, too, and fiddlers would play, and stories would be told, and you'd hear lots of laughter and get wonderful things to eat. There were good parties in those days.

Mrs. Lipscomb Wouldn't Like It

Did you see the story in the paper? Grocery chains are testing a procedure they call self-checking. That means the customers check their own groceries by passing each item across an electronic scanner. Then they get a total and go pay at a cashier's window.

I'm not sure I'll like that but I might.

Back when self-service began at filling stations, I didn't like pumping my own gas, for a while. But I ended up doing it and preferring it. At first I thought the oil companies were tricking me into doing work that their hired hands ought to be doing. I wasn't much impressed by the discount I got on self-service.

My trouble is, I remember this: When gasoline was selling for twenty-five cents a gallon, I would roll into a station and the guys working the driveway would check my radiator, my battery, my oil, my belts, and my tires. They would clean all the glass, from the headlights to the windshield to the side windows to the taillights, and they would sweep out the floorboards and empty the ashtrays. Then they would fill my tank with gas and the cost would be maybe three dollars. Once you have operated in times like those, it's not a joyful experience to pump your own gas at twenty dollars per tank, and get no service.

However, I am now a confirmed self-server at gas stations. The reason is that I began to have bad experiences from driveway help. Too many gas caps left on top of the car. I even had a kid leave the oil dipstick lying across my engine. It seemed to me the full-serve help went sour as soon as self-serve began.

So maybe I'll learn to prefer checking my own groceries, too.

You see what we're moving toward, on groceries. You'll go in a store and gather your stuff and check it out and maybe the only human you'll contact will be the cashier.

The next step will be the elimination of the cashier. I suppose eventually we'll pay for groceries by shoving a plastic card into a slot. Then it'll be possible to go to the grocery store without speaking to or dealing with anybody who works there.

All these changes tend to eliminate human contact. Conversation, especially. I bought a tank of gas not long ago in a self-serve station. I presented my credit card to a woman held captive in a glass cage and she filled out the slip and when I signed it she said, "Umpf."

The telephone company, which makes a living out of talk, last week sent me a plastic card to help me avoid talking to the operator. I've always liked talking to telephone operators. Some of my best friends are telephone operators. But I can see the telephone company doesn't want me talking to them.

The idea of self-checking groceries makes me remember Mrs. Lipscomb, back in my old hometown.

I had this Saturday job at the grocery store. One of my duties was to help the customers. Mrs. Lipscomb—I am calling her that because I am fairly sure it was her name—would show up with her grocery list on Saturday afternoon and she would never penetrate the store. I mean she would stand by the front door and visit while I gathered up her groceries.

She would say, "All right, get me a can of green beans."

I would go get the beans and she'd say, "All right, get me a can of cream corn."

She'd say, "All right, go back there and tell Mr. Meek I want a shoulder roast for tomorrow and tell him Wanda and her bunch are coming."

So I'd bring the roast, big enough for Wanda and her bunch, and Mrs. Lipscomb would say:

"All right, go back there again and tell him I need a pound of liver and I want it sliced thin."

This would last an hour, one item at a time. When she got all her stuff, I would walk home with her and carry it. Car? What car? She didn't have a car. She lived four blocks from the square where the store was and she expected delivery and she got it.

It's lucky for the grocery industry that the nation is no longer populated by Mrs. Lipscombs. Self-checking? You think Mrs. Lipscomb would check her own groceries? She wouldn't even *touch* them until I sat them down in her kitchen.

VII

THE WAY WE ARE

"Um," Cecil Said

His name is Cecil and he is chief cook and proprietor of the Highway Cafe, which serves hamburgers and plate lunches and T-bone steaks. Catfish on Fridays. Meatloaf on Wednesdays. Fried chicken on Sundays.

It was the quiet time of the day, when the lunch crowd had cleared out and the afternoon coffee drinkers hadn't yet begun to show. Cecil was taking the nearest thing he ever takes to a break. He was on a stool, slumped low, behind the cash register. He looked out the front window and across the highway but his eyes said they weren't seeing. Instead they were resting. People who run places like Cecil's always have tired eyes.

I asked if he thought it was getting colder.

"Um," he said. Cecil often responds to questions and comments with that "um." I'm not sure what it means.

Only other person in the place was a red-faced gent wearing a big hat and reading a newspaper. I could tell from the way the paper was folded that he was looking at the market report. By market report I don't mean the prices of shares on the New York Stock Exchange. I mean the prices of feeder steers and slaughter cows at Fort Worth, and Sealy, and Omaha.

Fellow in the big hat got up and cleared his throat and said to Cecil, "You got a twenty-dollar bill in that register I could borrow?"

Cecil opened the register and the cowman took the bill, without saying thanks. He had a toothpick in the corner of his mouth. He went out and got in a pickup and drove away slow. I remarked to Cecil that he sure seemed generous with his twenty-dollar bills. Could anybody get one, just by asking?

"Um," Cecil said. "Old Jim's good for it, don't worry. Got more money in the bank than he'll ever spend. He just don't like to take much of it out at a time. He'll be back in here for supper tonight and bring the twenty dollars. Probably he needs to buy gas, and doesn't want to go to the bank first."

Phone rang and Cecil picked it up and said, "CA-fay."

I thought of a company I called the other day and the person who answered began by identifying the firm, which has a lineup of four or five partners in its name, and next she thanked me for calling, and then asked if she could help me. I thought of that young woman, having to sit there and say all that when the phone rang, hundreds of times every day. I expect she would be envious of Cecil and his way of answering with that "CA-fay."

"Naw," he was saying now to the caller, "meatloaf's Wednesday." Then he said "um" and hung up.

We went back to Jim, the cowman. I told Cecil that I never had figured out how to look at a man in the country and tell whether he's got money. In the city I can pretty well do it, by the way he dresses and by what he drives and owns. But in a country town, the fellow with the holiest boots and the ugliest dog may have the most money.

Cecil nodded, just once, and said, "Well, in old Jim's case, it's just that he can't get *used* to having money. He never even saw many twenty-dollar bills until he was damn near fifty years old, then all of a sudden he was what you could call rich, around here."

Oil on his land?

"Um. Naw. Some big outfit in Dallas bought his ranch a couple of years back. Jim grew up on that old place, about 350 acres along the highway, few miles north of town. It's mostly just a bunch of brush. Ain't no way a man's gonna make a decent living in the cow business on that place, without he spent a fortune on improvements.

"But when Jim's daddy and mama died, at least he had the place, the land, and it was free and clear, and here came that bunch out of Dallas and paid him $3,000 an acre for it. Well, figure it up, what he got. It's more than a million bucks. Um."

I said I was surprised he didn't go buy him another ranch and Cecil said, "He's always threatenin' to do that but I tell him if he just needs to lose all his money, he don't have to buy no ranch. I'll sell him a CA-fay if he's itchin' to be broke again."

I paid for my coffee and got up to leave. Told Cecil to have a merry Christmas. "Um," he said.

The Way You'll Look

If you happen to be around thirty years old and if you're curious about the kind of person you'll be when you start getting Social Security, take a look at your mama and papa. In another thirty-five years, you're almost certain to be showing some of their present characteristics.

If they're not alive, even their photographs will give you some strong hints.

Studying parents can be of considerable value and great interest. I've only just begun to do it in recent times, and I wish I'd started sooner.

The last trip I made out to my old hometown, I was sitting in a little cafe, and something truly special happened. My mother walked in the front door.

Now that dear lady has been dead since 1958, and yet there she was walking toward me, waving and smiling, and for a couple of seconds I thought, well, this is a perfect miracle.

That person was my sister, of course, not our mother. But the resemblance jolted me. And the interesting thing is, it had never before struck me that these two people looked anything alike. I don't think they did, in fact, fifty years ago. So if you don't resemble your parents now, later on you may.

That little experience happened in October. Then in December I had an interesting note from one of the customers concerning the picture of me they're using now with this column. This gent was full of the Christmas spirit, I suppose, and was wanting to make me feel good, and he wrote that the picture looked like an old woman.

Well, maybe so. Like my sister, perhaps I am beginning to look like my mother, although I doubt it because she was not a bad-looking woman even when she was the age I am now. More likely it's my Aunt Carly I have come to resemble. The family always said Aunt Carly and my father favored each other. She was a schoolteacher up in the Panhandle and stood a solid six feet tall. I was always uncomfortable around her because she loomed. In my family we've always had a few large women who were loomers, who stood over us and frowned down, looming that way.

You may discover, as your birthdays accumulate, that you'll develop isolated physical similarities to one parent or another and not a general blanket resemblance.

Hands, for example, or necks, or stomachs, or ankles. Hasn't been long since I discovered a startling thing about the back of my neck. Before this happened I had never even *thought* about the back of my neck. Why would I want to?

Than I moved into an apartment that had a curious arrangement of bathroom mirrors. One morning when I was shaving, the mirror on the medicine cabinet behind me came open and presented, in the mirror over the sink, a close-up view of the back of my neck. I was amazed. Because it was my father's neck.

It had a peculiar pattern of wrinkles. Wait. Not wrinkles but creases, little canyons in the skin, and they were arranged in a cross-hatch pattern, similar to the way cooks take a knife and score a flounder before it's broiled.

Well, I can say I have reproduced the back of my father's neck, just exactly, and it wasn't any strain at all because I didn't know I had done it. I like it. I like the back of my neck now a lot better than the front.

If you're laughing at me, just wait. All this will happen to you, too, and you won't laugh then.

Not just physical stuff. You may *hear* things you thought you'd never again hear. I heard my father laugh the other night. What do you think of that? It was his laugh, don't worry. I heard it a thousand times when I was growing up in his house. The laugh came out of me.

For the first time, I was able to hear that I was giving off the same sound he did when he laughed. I wasn't happy about that. I always thought he laughed too loud, and the sound had a tinny quality produced too high in the throat and it was not pleasant.

So from now on I intend to watch how I laugh. Also what I get angry about. And what I count to be important. I believe we can learn so much from the lives of our parents.

All this teaching from our mothers and fathers (after six decades of life, in my case), I count it a rite of becoming old. It's like growing up again.

Moving vs. Staying

Few days ago, for a reason I don't remember now, I mentioned here that I had moved. I have been surprised that the casual mention of moving has brought so much comment from the customers. I don't mean they are commenting about my own move, but about theirs. Everybody has a story about moving.

Houston is a city of moving folks. Look in the phone directory. You'll find thirty full Yellow Pages devoted to listings and ads for household movers.

Peoples' lives consist mainly of one ordinary event after another, but moving is no such event. It's always extraordinary. My neighbor Chester Adams tells me he has counted up and found that he has lived in fourteen different houses in his life and he can remember the details of every one of those moves, even though the early ones came when he was a small child. He says something special happened during each of the moves to make it memorable.

Maybe that happens to everybody. The recent move I made was probably the shortest in my history. That is, I moved sixty steps down a hall, from one apartment to another. But what made it special was that just when I was about to go out and get somebody to help me move the heavy stuff that I couldn't handle alone, my son from Mobile, Alabama, walked in. He spent a day of his vacation helping me wrestle bookcases and filing cabinets.

We had a good time. Been nearly fifteen years since we worked together that way. There's something rewarding in doing a physical chore with a person you care about. Neither of you could do it alone but together you can, and it makes you both feel good.

My son is expert at moving. He has moved dozens and dozens of times. He grinned when he heard my neighbor Chester's remark about living in fourteen different houses. In our family, that's no mobility at all. We have always tended to keep on the go. This tendency traces back to times when our forebears were guided by the principle that a moving target is harder to hit than a stationary one.

Somewhere in the family, then, we have always had one person who is a super-competent household mover. The son from Mobile (or wherever he happens to be parked) now occupies this position. He is skilled at getting large and weighty objects moved from one place to another at no cost whatever. He also knows the secret of how to get a dresser twenty-six inches wide through a twenty-four-inch opening. It has to do with dismantling door frames, and things like that. It involves pinchbars and loud splintering noises. When it begins, I go out for hamburgers and beer.

Changing dwelling places frequently gives people handy reference points, in reviewing their lives. My bunch has always been able to pinpoint an event in the past by saying, "It happened when we were living in the Nichols house in Glen Rose. I'm sure of that because the way he broke his leg was falling over the pump in the backyard and that's the only place we ever lived that had a pump in the backyard."

All right, it's for sure that we didn't live in that house, or any other, much more than a year. So that narrows the search for the date of an event. These things are of value, provided you have any interest in family history.

I know people as old as I am who are still living in the house where they were born. I've had them take me out on the screened porch in back to show me the pencil marks their parents made on the door frame, when they were measuring the height of growing offspring.

"This is how tall I was when I was six," they'll say. "And here's how tall I was when I was ten. And here's when I graduated from high school."

In my family we didn't do that because we knew, without talking about it, that we wouldn't be in the same house when anybody graduated from high school.

I never have decided which is better—to grow up all in one place, or move around.

At one time I believed it was better to stay put, and be able to see every day all your memories. When you were forty you could look out the window and see the chinaberry tree you fell out of and broke your arm when you were eleven years old.

And the president of the bank would be somebody who knew your father, and fished with him. The aging English teacher in the high school, who taught you when you were a senior, would also teach your children and they would make better grades on account of it. You would have permanency, roots, and that can be a good thing. Give you a strong sense of who you are, what your purpose is.

But now I'm not sure about that. The world is changing too fast now for that to be the advantage I once thought it was. I meet people who call themselves military brats. They moved every time anybody cut a set of orders that said their parents were to leave San Antonio and report on 26 July to Newport News, Virginia. People who grew up that way seem pretty well prepared for the way the world is now, the way it's changing so fast. Maybe it's better to be movers instead of stayers.

Some people may not be certain which they are, movers or stayers-put. My personal system of judging is based on ten-year intervals. If you've averaged one change of dwelling place every decade, I say you're a stayer. Anything above that, you show tendencies of the old itchin' foot.

Personally I overqualify as a mover. I was getting nervous in that previous place because I'd been there four years. My average, over more than half a century, is less than two years per house. Can you beat that?

Beautiful Places to Live

One of the customers called to tell me about a place in New Mexico where she is about to move. The house she'll live in is up the side of a mountain and when she sits on the front porch she can see a stream glittering in the valley, miles below. She said when the aspens are golden in the fall, the view from her porch is the most beautiful she's ever seen. And now, just think of it, she will get to go and live there.

What brought me that phone call was a little description I had in the paper about the view from an imaginary house up in that Grand Prairie country southwest of Fort Worth. I have often fantasized about living there, if I could pick my spot, and I still enjoy thinking about it. But even in my most creative daydreams, the view from that porch has not been the most beautiful I've ever seen, or even near it.

I would be mighty cautious about moving to the most beautiful place I've ever seen. I'm afraid I'd destroy it.

Sometimes I try to establish in my head the place I've seen that's the most beautiful, and I keep going back to California. I am talking about natural beauty, not buildings or gardens or other person-made things.

To show you that place, I would have to take you to the coast of northern California where the redwoods grow almost to the cliffs of the Pacific shore. Now add a sunset to those redwoods, or put a full moon over the ocean swells breaking against the great rocks at the foot of the cliffs—the magnificence of the scenery is almost overwhelming.

But to live there? To have a house on that coast? And come home every night to all that natural splendor going on in my front yard? I don't believe so. I'm afraid that in six weeks I wouldn't think it was extraordinary any longer, and might go looking for something better.

Old friend Morgan, who lives down at Freeport, tried to explain this very problem to me, years ago before I'd ever thought of it. He was in love with the Mexican city of Monterrey. Not so much because it's so beautiful but because he always felt good there. He was living and working in Mexico then and had the option of locating his office and home just about anywhere in the north part of the republic.

I asked him why not Monterrey? If he thought it was the best place on the planet to be, if he went there every chance he got, why not move there? He said, "Oh, I wouldn't ever do that. If I lived in Monterrey, I couldn't go there to visit."

He'd lose it, is what he was saying, if he stayed permanently in a place he loved so much to visit.

When my masters at the *Chronicle* bought me a ticket to San Francisco for the 1984 Democratic National Convention, I went to a party there. It was in a home on one of those hills. The guests came just before sunset. The host handed us a glass of wine and let us go out on his deck to watch the day end.

My guilt-ridden Protestant upbringing whispered to me that it was probably sinful to be in such a pleasant circumstance. Standing there on a platform overlooking one of the world's most beautiful cities. Watching the remarkable show of changing light—both natural and otherwise—that goes on almost constantly over San Francisco Bay.

I had to wonder what all that beautifulness meant to the multitudes who live on those hills and can look out their windows at any time and take in the show. Do they get tired of it? Does the beauty fade? Are their spirits renewed and uplifted, every day, when they look out their back doors?

The host addressed that matter briefly. His theory is that people are not made happy simply by moving into a beautiful place, if they imagine that living with natural beauty is the key to happiness. That is, if dissatisfied people live in a dreary place, and if they are convinced the dreariness is the source of their discontent, moving to a beautiful place is not likely to make them suddenly happy. Because, once they've moved, they can no longer blame their unhappiness on the place they live.

You may not be able to take that theory to the bank and get any cash for it but I have seen it work, many times. Not in San Francisco but here at home. I know a host of folks who are convinced that once they leave the heat and congestion and pollution of Houston, and get into a little country house somewhere on the bank of a pretty stream, they will be happy at last. I've also seen a lot of them return after a couple of years. The ones who go, and stay, and get happy may be more numerous than I imagine and I hope they are.

For many years I thought that what I needed, in order to become a better writer (meaning a more successful one who made a lot of money) was a place of beauty to work in. I thought if I lived on a mountain, I would be continually inspired by the beauty of my surroundings and I would grind out best-selling prose with everlasting life. I see now I was wrong. I am better off looking out my apartment window at a solid board fence. And being inspired by the knowledge that if I keep working, maybe I can return to a beautiful place I remember in California, Canada, or Scotland.

What Are They Looking At?

At Hallettsville I turned off the highway and circled the Lavaca County courthouse a couple of times. I wanted to show one of my favorite old Texas buildings to a friend who was riding with me.

On a corner of the square, half a dozen men were standing around an old pickup, looking down into the bed. The friend riding with me was fascinated by the way all six of the men stood perfectly still, their heads bowed toward the truck bed.

That scene didn't hold a lot of interest for me because it's a common one in rural Texas.

I drove on back to the highway and the friend said, "I'd think you'd be curious about what's in the back of that truck."

I said I already knew what was in the truck and it wasn't anything I cared to see. It was a big catfish, not quiet dead. It would be lying there giving off a gasp now and then.

"How do you know that?"

I know it from standing on a hundred courthouse squares and looking down into truck beds. If it's not a fish it's a big dead snake. But I figure it's a little early for the snake so it's a fish, caught on a trotline or a throwline out of the Lavaca River. If not the Lavaca then the Navidad or the Guadalupe.

"Why is it brought to town?" the friend asked.

Because it weighs at least thirty-five pounds and needs to be shown. Sometimes you'll see a fish of fifty pounds. Or even seventy-five or eighty, but a fish of that size is rare and draws a large crowd.

The only other thing that might be lying in that pickup is a big dead wolf. It won't be a wolf but it'll be called a wolf. It'll be part coyote and part dog and it'll be of really impressive size or else it wouldn't be brought to town to show.

There are exceptions to these rules but they occur so rarely they're worth only a brief mention. Instead of a catfish in the truck it could be a great turtle caught out of the river. But it will need to be a turtle the size of a washtub or nobody will pay it any attention.

This bringing to town of caught fish and slain snakes is related to the practice of bringing in for display extraordinary produce grown on area farms. For example, the outsized watermelon.

When I migrated to the Gulf Coast area shortly after World War II, farmers were still trying to grow watermelons as big as possible. In those times, when you saw men standing around a pickup in town, they might be looking at a watermelon weighing eighty-seven pounds.

Bigness, in the matter of farm products, was associated with quality. In watermelons, especially.

About this time, the late Landon Bradshaw of Jasper raised an East Texas watermelon that weighed 136 pounds and Landon became temporarily famous across the country. That notoriety was due to his appearance on the network television show "I've Got a Secret."

The viewers of that program probably supposed that Landon was getting rich, raising giant watermelons. The fact was, a mighty small market existed for 136-pound watermelons. No housewife wanted a melon she couldn't lift, and even a half of the thing wouldn't fit inside her refrigerator.

But we clung fiercely to the notion that bigness meant quality. For one thing, it was fun.

It was also an old idea, as old as man himself. Among ancient people, the fellow who speared the biggest fish became a big man in the clan. I can see him bringing that fish to the mouth of the cave and flinging it down (since he didn't have a pickup to display it in), as everybody came forth to admire it.

Early in the 1930s, my Uncle John Campbell somehow raised a giant elongated squash up in Palo Pinto County. I don't know whether he did it on purpose. Maybe it was some kind of genetic accident. But that squash grew to something like four feet. It was slender and slightly hooked at one end. Then it got thicker gradually and bulged at the bottom. Some squash.

Uncle John took it into Gordon, which is a little town on the T&P Railroad where he traded. He went in and out of stores with that squash on his shoulder like he was carrying a rifle.

He wasn't trying to sell the thing. He was just showing it, like a fifty-pound catfish or an eighty-pound watermelon is shown. To me the good thing was that Uncle John had fun with that great squash, hearing people exclaim, watching their mouths fly open. But there was no market for a four-foot squash, no more than for a 136-pound watermelon.

That doesn't keep such wonders from being interesting, though. Country editors have always printed pictures of big dead snakes and their slayers. Also pictures of great catfish and their catchers.

Recently I was reading the *Diboll Free Press* from up in Angelina County and editor Paul Durham seemed to be reminding readers of his paper's big-snake policy. He said the *Free Press* would be pleased to publish pictures of impressive rattlesnakes. He said nobody had brought in a big snake in a good while and he just wanted to remind subscribers that snakes are welcome at the newspaper office, provided they are already dead.

Next time you pass through Hallettsville, which is on U.S. 90A about halfway between Houston and San Antonio, you might want to take a look at that courthouse square. It's one of the best in Texas. I don't promise you'll see a pickup with a big fish in it, but you might.

Valuable Notes Retrieved

Monday was a good day for me because I found a notebook I'd lost. It contained some messages I'd written to myself.

One was a reminder to tell you about Otto Whittington's green mules.

Another was about Dan Griffin's wonderful method of repelling little kids that get on his nerves.

Another concerned what Martha Ann Walls' mother said about the Houston telephone book.

All these are important things, and it scares me to think how close I came to forgetting them.

Almost any information about a mule is of interest to me so I paid close attention when Otto Whittington told me about these green mules in the Philippines, not long after Pearl Harbor. He became one of the "Battlin' Bastards of Bataan," but when the war began, Whittington was a corporal in the army's Veterinary Corps and assigned to a jungle animal hospital on Bataan. The army was still using horses and mules in the Philippines then, and a couple of near-white Missouri mules showed up in this hospital. They needed treatment for wounds from Japanese fragmentation bombs.

The air over Bataan was full of Japanese planes, and the white mules were easy to see from the air. Low-flying Zero pilots would empty their guns on that little vet hospital area, mainly because the white mules drew their attention.

So the commanding officer ordered Whittington to camouflage those mules. He dyed them green.

He got twenty-four packets of Putnam dye from a quartermaster dump and mixed it in a fifty-five-gallon drum and made great swabs out of gunny sacks and turned those mules green.

His commanding officer was pleased and invited all West Pointers in the area to come and inspect the only green mules ever to serve in the U.S. Army.

I wanted to get that in the paper because I am afraid it wouldn't be recorded anywhere else.

Otto Whittington came originally from Sweetwater, out the other side of Abilene. He lives now in Houston.

Dan Griffin does, too. He has done something even more wonderful.

Griffin and I have never sat at the same table to drink a cup of coffee, or anything else, but I know we would get along first-rate.

He is sometimes troubled by what he calls "obstreperous children." I share this trouble with Griffin. I have had it ever since the Age of Child Worship began, which I think was somewhere around 1945.

My dictionary states that "obstreperous" means "noisily and stubbornly defiant" or "aggressively boisterous." Yes.

I would add the awkward phrase "attention-seeking inquisitiveness." Such as when adults are minding their personal matters and little kids come up and stick their noses in and ask questions or make comments that are not any of their business.

A long time ago I composed a certain sentence to speak to a nosy kid giving me trouble in public. I can't recall whether I ever told you about it. It is a powerful sentence.

I have now refined it down to nine extraordinary words. When I put that sentence into a kid's ear, he is immobilized. He stops whatever he's doing that wigs me and walks away, slowly, looking back in wonder.

And he doesn't go tell his mama or papa what I said, either. He doesn't want them to know that he has even *heard* such a thing.

No, I can't put my sentence in the paper. It's too powerful. I wouldn't trust the general public with it. In the wrong hands it could do serious damage to nice little children who know how to behave.

My sentence does have a weakness: I can't deliver it unless I have the target isolated. That is, I can't plant it in the head of a child in the presence of his parents. If I did, they would sue me.

I could win the case, because no judge or jury would ever dispute that the application of these words is anything but beneficial to the recipient. However, I don't want lawsuits. Takes too much time.

Now then, Dan Griffin's system is better than mine. No words are involved. He uses "a muscular twitch invisible to others." Then he adds "a slight exhalation."

This may be the greatest understatement I have ever heard. Griffin provided photographs to demonstrate his method. They aren't anything short of diabolical. I wouldn't put them in the paper. The editors wouldn't use them, anyway. Some things are beyond public acceptance, no matter how useful they may be.

The greatest feature of Griffin's system is that he does not need to be devious about using it, as I am about mine. He doesn't isolate the target. He can, as he says, apply his method, "in the presence of the parents without their knowledge."

This is powerful medicine.

With his dreadful facial twitch and the snarl (or whatever it is) that follows, Griffin claims he has "transformed (misbehaving children) into silent, quivering mounds of terror."

Now that's a contribution that society needs. But I don't suppose society could handle it, any better than they could handle my sentence.

The third matter:

Mary Ann Walls' mother was visiting in Houston when her daughter went out to get the telephone directory left on her step. She dragged it in by its plastic cover, and her mother said: "I don't believe I'd like to live in a place where I couldn't pick up the phone book."

◆————————————————◆

The Many Faces of a State

A few days ago I talked on the phone to a New York fellow who is interested in locations for shooting a movie in our state. He asked me to tell him what the countryside was like.

I tried to make him understand that describing the surface of Texas in a few words is not easy and he said, "Well, just look out the window and tell me what you see."

At that moment I was in a motel in Nacogdoches. I looked out the window and decided not to tell him that what I saw was the brick wall of a Chinese restaurant. People in the East have their special notions of what this state looks like, and they are not going to accept that we can look out windows and see Chinese restaurants. They had rather we saw cactus and oil derricks and bunkhouses.

So instead of the restaurant I tried to describe the campus of Stephen F. Austin State University. I could not see that campus from the window, but it's only a few blocks from the motel. Its buildings are set in a magnificent forest, mostly pine trees.

I don't believe that description suited the film-making gent any better than the Chinese restaurant would have. It's practically impossible for New Yorkers who've never seen Texas to accept that it has forests. Or even universities, except on Saturdays when we play football.

The reason I thought of the phone call is, I believe that fellow would like what I am seeing now. It's more in keeping with our state's national image.

I'm sitting just below a rocky ridge, a few miles east of the Panhandle city of Canyon, and looking out over a rugged valley with a stream running through it. Above the rim of the opposite ridge, to the south, the land is given mainly to ranching and so flat I expect I'm seeing objects twenty miles away. The canyon floor is covered in trees but certainly not pines. I think they're mostly elms.

Anyway, the distance from Nacogdoches to this Panhandle canyon, the way I came, is close to 600 miles. I came out of the Piney Woods and drove west across the sandhills of the Post Oak Belt. Through the neat farms of the Texas Blacklands. Then the scrubby trees of the West Cross Timbers. Onto the gentle slopes of the Rolling Plains, to climb the Caprock onto the Staked Plains and then north into the Panhandle.

Even that sketchy route would probably have given the New York fellow more than he wanted to hear about Texas. Each of those regions has its own distinctions, and there are several others I didn't mention.

We often associate the Panhandle with unhappy climate—heat and wind and sand and blizzards—but when this country's weather is good, like now, it blesses Panhandle people with exquisite days, cool and bright and calm. I had almost forgotten the experience of inhaling and not smelling anything in the air.

Unless I'm reading my map wrong, the stream below me is Tierra Blanca Creek. The water passing here will flow into Palo Duro Creek and then into the great canyon of that same name.

Palo Duro Canyon is probably a dozen miles southeast of this spot. It's always seemed a curiosity to me that some of the most spectacular natural scenery in Texas is up here in the Panhandle, which most of us visualize as an unbroken plain.

Once you've seen Palo Duro you never again think of the High Texas Plains as unbroken. This stream dug a ditch—in places more than 1,000 feet deep—across 120 miles of the Panhandle and in this state you'd have to go to the Big Bend Country to see natural scenery as rugged as Palo Duro.

Look here, on the map, at one of the oddest placenames in Texas. The stream that dug Palo Duro Canyon answers to the name Prairie Dog Town Fork of the Red River. I am tempted to call that New York movie fellow and tell him about this river. With a name like that, it's probably just the place he's looking for.

"Will Work for Food"

She came up to my car in the parking lot at the supermarket and asked if I had any work she could do, like cleaning house, or washing clothes. She said she would work for meals.

The pitch interested me because a month earlier I saw it being used up in Fort Worth, at a traffic light on a feeder off Interstate 35. A fellow who looked in his mid-thirties stood on an overpass and held up a sign to motorists who stopped for the light. Sign was printed on a square of cardboard. It read, "Will Work for Food."

The light caught me and I got a chance to look the guy over pretty close. Something about him bothered me. I decided he didn't look hungry. He had a beard that was neat-trimmed. He hadn't slept the night before in an alley or a ditch. He was organized.

I watched a woman beckon to him and hand out a twenty-dollar bill. He said to her, "Do you know of any work?" Woman said no, she was from Houston and didn't know about jobs in Fort Worth. The man thanked her for the money and said, "If you hear of anybody who has work, I wish you'd send them around." Send them around to his office, there at I-35 and Berry.

I was able to hear this conversation because the woman who contributed the twenty dollars was in the car with me. I told her I thought she had been conned. She said maybe so but she liked the idea of a guy making the public announcement that he was willing to work for food.

Just as the light changed, a man in a pickup behind me waved two bills. The fellow with the sign faded back there, stepping quick and nimble, and took the money. I couldn't see the denomination of the bills.

But the guy had picked up twenty-two dollars, at the least, on one red light. Not too bad. I wondered how much he might collect on a good day, standing out there with his sign.

So I thought of him again when the woman spoke to me in the parking lot about working for meals. She seemed about fifty. Had on a kind of pantsuit. Carried a drawstring purse that looked a little too good. A fleshy round face with one of those smoker's mouths that has the vertical crevasses in the upper lip.

I asked if five dollars would help her and she said it sure would. I got out a bill and asked, before I handed it over, if she got many jobs working for food.

"Some," she said.

How many times, say in the past month, had she worked for food?

"Not many."

Six times?

"Well, no, not six."

Twice?

She almost laughed. "Okay, twice." She looked at the bill, as if she thought it was time I gave it to her.

Instead I asked her name.

"Are you law?" She looked in my car.

Told her no, not law, just an ordinary taxpayer.

She said, "My name's Mary."

Mary, oh boy, now that's distinctive. I bet I could have yelled, "Hey, Mary!" there in the parking lot and a dozen women would have turned to see who was calling them.

I told Mary about the fellow in Fort Worth with the sign, and how he picked up the twenty-two dollars in less than a minute. She seemed interested, and got a mentholated cigarette out of the drawstring purse and fired up with one of those little disposable lighters.

I checked her shoes. I have this theory that shoes tell

a lot about financial circumstance, much more than clothing. I thought her shoes looked way too good.

"A sign wouldn't work," Mary said, "not for a woman. And you wouldn't ever catch me out on the freeway, and sure not with a sign. In this town? Wouldn't be five minutes before you'd have a cop talking to you."

She seemed more relaxed so I went ahead and asked how much cash she got on an average day, offering to work for meals.

The questions made her angry, or seemed to, and for a couple of seconds I thought she was going to walk away from the five-dollar bill. She didn't, though.

"Look buddy," she said, "I'm not working any kind of game. I'm like a lot of other people right now. I'm down, you know? I'm just trying to make it, that's all."

Would she really work for meals?

"Damn right."

How about today, right now? Would she go to my place and clean it up if I gave her dinner?

She was shaking her head before I got the question out, and I felt she had heard that challenge before. "No, not today. I can't go right now because I've got things to do."

I didn't ask what things she had to do. Figured she wouldn't tell me. Probably what she had to do was work that parking lot, offering to clean houses in return for meals.

Before she walked away she did take the five dollars. What do you think about her?

Flo and Jim

"You know where I'd be right now," she said, "if I'd married Jim?" She had brought a kitchen towel to the booth. She wiped her face and the back of her neck and pulled cigarettes from the pocket of her apron. She look tired.

"I'd be living in one of those high-rise condos on the west side of town. One of those deals where you buy an entire floor for a million bucks and then they finish it up inside the way you want it. That's where I'd be living. I'd be Miz Gotrocks. I'd probably be going to charity balls."

Jim's living in a high-rise now?

She nodded. "He sold that mansion or whatever you call it. Looked like a Ramada Inn. From what I hear now about real estate, it's almost impossible to sell a big house like that for half what it cost. Well, Jim put it on the market and sold it in two months for exactly what he asked. Isn't that like him? He's doing everything just that way."

I suppose, then, that she hears from him, that they keep in touch.

She shook her head. "Naw, not direct. But I hear. You want your coffee warmed?"

She slid out of the booth, and for an instant I saw in her movement a glimmer of the grace and beauty she had back in school long ago. Best dancer on the floor, we always said.

She must be sixty-two now, maybe sixty-three, an age when so many of us realize our lives are not ever going to be much different or at least not any better. A time for examining mistakes.

She came back to the booth with the hot coffee.

"You want to hear something good? Ask me why I didn't marry Jim."

All right, why didn't she? Everyone certainly thought they'd marry. They were a pair, Flo and Jim, Jim and Flo. We seldom said one name without the other.

"My mother talked me out of it," she said. "Mama thought he was too short for me. Actually, when we got engaged, Jim *was* about an inch shorter, and Mama said 'Flo, don't ever marry a man shorter than you are. All your life you'll be wearing flats and they'll make your legs look bad. Go out and find yourself a man you can look up to,' she said. 'You need a real man who'll amount to something.' That's my mother, giving me her best advice. Oh boy."

I decided not to comment on that. We sat a minute and watched the traffic. The place was quiet during the mid-afternoon slow time that comes to most little restaurants.

"When I gave Jim back my ring and broke things off, I figured he'd throw a fit. He didn't. He just said 'I don't know why you're doing this but it's a mistake and I'll give you time to find that out.'

"And every month, for a year, he'd call to see if I'd changed my mind. He'd already started his company then and was going all over. He'd call from California, Pennsylvania, Canada, everywhere, and ask me to take the ring back."

Well, why didn't she take it back and marry him?

She stared at me a few seconds and then said quietly, "I don't know. I wish I had. I guess because of Lew. You never met Lew."

No.

"When Lew and I got engaged, Jim called me and he said 'Flo, don't marry that guy. You don't love him and it'll be a disaster.' Boy, was he ever right.

"Lew wasn't really my husband. He was more my mother's. Mama was crazy about him. Big dude, and beautiful, and he never grew up. Never got off the bottle. I spent twelve tough years trying to make an adult out of him."

She divorced him then?

"Yes."

And then did she get in touch with Jim, let him know she was free?

A slow shake of her head. "No, because it was too late. He was already married."

We went silent again for a while and then her face lifted and she said, "He was in here once. Couple of years ago."

Jim was? In the restaurant?

"Yeah, sat right over there. Slumming, I guess. I didn't speak to him. He was with a pretty woman. His wife, I suppose. But I found out something."

What was that?

"He's grown, some way. He's taller than I am now. Isn't that funny?"

She gave me a light hug.

"Well, I've got to go poke my stove," she said and disappeared into the kitchen of that little restaurant where she works.

♦———————————————————♦

A Risky Target

It's Wednesday morning, eight o'clock. Washday at my place. I've got two loads on rinse cycle now and two more waiting. Woman's work is never done.

One good thing about washing this way is that I don't need to worry about breaking the pot.

I seldom do laundry without thinking of the time I broke the wash pot. I committed that felony long ago but I am getting so I remember ancient history much better than recent.

For example, about two hours ago I picked up a roll of quarters off the top of the radio and laid it down in another place. That's the recent history. What I can't remember about the event is where I put the quarters down.

They may turn up a week from now in some curious place. On a dark closet shelf, maybe, or in the refrigerator. I once found my wallet in the refrigerator after it had been missing two days.

Losing the quarters caused me to go to the store for change. Because where I live, you can't wash without quarters. Seventy-five cents per washer load, and the same for the dryer. So I shell out $4.50 in quarters every week, for four loads in the washing machines and two in the dryer. I'm glad my Methodist mother doesn't know that. She wouldn't accept $4.50 a week as a reasonable cost to keep clothes clean.

I expect that amount would have bought her a new wash pot to replace the one I broke. At the time I am talking about, $4.50 would have also paid her grocery bill for a week.

Did you ever do a forbidden thing, without ever understanding why you did it? That's how I broke the wash pot. I picked up a good solid rock and heaved it and by some incredible stroke of misfortune that rock struck the cast-iron post in a sensitive place and broke it.

I can remember exactly the sound the pot produced when the rock struck. It was both beautiful and dreadful. I mean it was a really nice throw from a respectable range, with a rock of considerable heft. That was the beautiful part. I don't have to tell you what was dreadful about it. That pot was valuable family equipment.

I decided not to go in and confess. It wasn't necessary.

They would discover the damage soon enough and I would hear about it before supper. I was always the principal suspect in crimes of this sort.

They came to me and they asked, "Did you break the wash pot?"

I said I wasn't sure. I thought they shouldn't expect a guilty person to make a confession on the first question. It wouldn't be natural.

"You're not sure?" they said. "How can you not be sure?"

There was no possible answer. At least not one that would satisfy them. I said I didn't know how I wasn't sure.

"Did you do it on purpose?" they asked next.

You can see, by the wording of that question, they already knew I was guilty. Why did they draw the examination out so long? It was like the questioning was part of the punishment.

I told them not exactly, that I didn't *exactly* break the wash pot on purpose.

There was no way they would understand the truth in that response, so I didn't try to explain it. I'm not sure I can even now, but I know it was at least partly an honest answer.

The wash pot was turned upside down on the rocks that it sat on when we built the fire beneath it on washday. It was an inviting target, with its bottom bulging. Presenting itself. Asking to be chunked at. Pleading, almost.

Sure, other targets were available. Washtubs. Lard buckets. Fence posts. Rain barrels.

But those carried no risk. Nobody paid any attention if you chunked a lard bucket. So I threw at the wash pot, which was important. And risky.

It's in the nature of humans to chunk wash pots. We go around all the time, passing up safe enterprises, looking for risk. I can't say why. It doesn't make a lot of sense. We throw at the wash pot, wanting to hit it because it'll give us a quiver of excitement. Yet, knowing that if we do, we're in trouble. What a strange form of life we are.

Excuse me now while I go switch my towels and undershirts from the washer to the dryer. Until I talk to you again, be careful what you throw rocks at.

And if you find a roll of quarters lying around, it's mine.

The Changing of a Mind

One of the customers sent me a clipping of something I wrote more than thirty years ago. Don't flinch, I am not going to reprint any of that old piece. It was bad and I am embarrassed to read it now and distressed to be reminded that copies of it are still floating around.

One of the risks you take in a job of this sort is that the very worst day's work you'll do in your entire career will be preserved unto eternity, world without end, amen. It may be lining a pantry shelf, or stuck down in the bottom of a trunk in an attic, or used as packing in a furniture warehouse. But it's there, always, and one day it will surface to confront you and say, "Look what *you* did in 1956."

But this customer, who asks that her name be left out of the paper, is not concerned about the quality of that old piece. What interests her is that it paraded an opinion I then had on the matter of mothers who have young children and who work outside the home. Customer says I have lately expressed a second opinion on the same subject and it's different. In fact, it is just the opposite. Her question is, "How do you reconcile these views?"

Well, I don't. The nearest I can come is to admit that I've changed my mind about working mothers.

In the last forty years I've changed my mind about so many matters, I would not recognize myself if you described me by what I thought when I was young. If you took me back to what I believed when I was eighteen, and forced me to live by those precepts, by now I would very likely be dead, or at least in jail.

Listen, when I was twenty I thought the greatest writer in America was Max Shulman. Does that tell you anything? Also I thought the sexiest woman alive was Carmen Miranda, and one of the finest songs ever written was "Dipsy Doodle."

When I was twenty-two, I seriously entertained the thought that the evils of this planet would be eliminated if we would simply do away with all Germans and Japanese, and restock Germany and Japan with nice people from America.

When I was twenty-four, I thought that all blonde women were stupid.

So let us now praise the changing of minds.

Goals change, too. Ambitions fade. Dreams die, and are resurrected in new forms. Everybody is different from the way they started out. This is what makes people interesting and mysterious and unpredictable.

Consider the political races, which everybody is considering right now despite that they may be sick to the stomach of them. I would not want to confess how many times I have changed my mind in the last several months about the ways I intend to vote next Tuesday on the various races.

Change? In thirty years? Why, I have changed in the last thirty days.

For almost twenty years, until I was something like forty-five, my goal in this life was to move to Mexico forever, somewhere around Saltillo or Durango in that desert country. I thought it would be wonderful to live a simple happy life down there in one of those little Mexican villages. If I had tried that, I'd never have been heard from again.

When I graduated from that notion, I took up wanting to move out to the Big Bend or the Davis Mountains, and live in an adobe house and sit beside a cactus and write best-selling novels. I stayed with that fantasy until a literary agent explained to me how few people in this country live off writing novels, and he convinced me to keep the newspaper job I had. That's about the only favor a literary agent ever did for me.

Personal customs change. Habits change. Tastes. Capabilities. I can't even sleep the way I once did. For my first forty years I slept on my stomach. Now I can't lie down that way for ten minutes because it hurts.

I always liked traveling in white cars, and bought one every two years until suddenly last spring I couldn't stand the notion of another white car, so I got a solid black one.

Only a couple of years ago, when I got truly hungry I went forth and ate one of three meals. I would get a big steak with the juices running out and a baked potato covered over with sour cream. Or I would get fried chicken with cream gravy poured over a mountain of mashed potatoes. Or I would get a great layout of beef enchiladas with orange cheese bubbling across their tops.

Now? Any one of those meals would make me sick. Two in succession would keep me up and groaning all night. Three in a row would put me into a hospital.

Also I wasted years of my life hating Monday mornings, and Monday has become one of my favorite days. Monday now suggests to me a new beginning, another chance, and I like the way it feels. The day I don't much care for now is Thursday.

Not Ready for Ironing

Without any warning I drove up to the home of a friend who has been living alone in a full-sized house ever since I've known him, which is something like twelve years. I had to knock twice and let out a yell before he knew I had come because he was running the vacuum cleaner and it makes a substantial racket.

I have watched this fellow develop into a pretty good housekeeper since a divorce sent him back into bachelorhood. He was just finishing up the living room with that vacuum sweeper and doing a smooth job. Among my friends are several ex-husbands and I have studied their habits. I can watch a guy operate a vacuum and tell you within a year how long he's been cleaning his own diggings. The new bachelors run a vacuum as if they're pushing a garden plow. The experienced ones are loose-wristed and graceful.

My friend unplugged the vacuum and wrapped its cord neatly and stored the machine away where it's supposed to stay. Then he got out the ironing board and said, "Sit down a minute while I iron a couple of shirts."

The house looked nice. Everything in its proper place. Windows clean. Furniture dusted. And the carpets were splendid. Nothing makes a house look so cared for as a freshly vacuumed carpet, with the nap standing at attention. Makes you afraid to walk on it because you don't want to leave tracks. It's like a yard covered in snow, which begs you not to step on it.

But ironing a shirt, now there's a test. When an ex-husband has learned to iron a shirt, he's pretty well down the path to permanent bachelorhood.

I sat and watched and made the old joke about how

woman's work is never done and he said, "Actually, I've gotten so I enjoy taking care of my house. I get in here on Saturday morning and sometimes I spend four or five hours cleaning and fixing and when I get through, everything looks so nice it makes me feel good."

I tried to figure out whether I knew what he was saying. I think now I do. I've had similar symptoms. However, I don't believe I'm anywhere near as close as he is to total conversion to housekeeping.

But you can find books written by hairy-chested men who don't mind admitting they enjoy keeping house. About forty years ago a gent named Roy Bedichek wrote a book, *Adventures with a Texas Naturalist*, while living alone for a year on Friday Mountain Ranch west of Austin. The book was published in New York in 1948 and is now counted a classic in Texas letters.

I have never thought it's such a great book but I've loved it for one reason—its introduction. I don't believe I ever loved any other book for that reason.

In the intro, Bedichek wrote about where he stayed during that year, and how he lived. He discovered he liked doing the work necessary to feed himself and maintain his living quarters. He said the same thing my shirt-ironing friend said, but not in the same words: "My little household duties amuse me and furnish a refuge in reality," Bedichek wrote. "Doing my own chores gives me a sense of independence and of satisfaction . . . "

His "little household duties" may insult a multitude of homemakers, but I came to understand what he felt out there on that ranch.

Few years ago when I got cast adrift (for the same reason the ironer of the shirts did), I learned to appreciate the sense of independence and satisfaction that Bedichek found in cooking his own stew, making his bed, sweeping his floors.

I haven't yet found so much satisfaction in it that I

keep my premises manicured the way my shirt-ironing friend does. But I have learned a thing or two. One is that if I go off on a trip and leave my premises in a mess, it makes a bad homecoming. Once I returned and found the place so torn up I thought somebody had broken in and wrecked it, when in fact I was the one who had wrecked it by packing for the trip. Since then I have left it in a little better condition, and this makes me gladder to get home. Sometimes I am truly surprised to walk into an orderly place. So maybe I am getting better.

But ironing shirts, I don't know about that. I'm sure I have an iron because I remember seeing it somewhere. However, I haven't actually plugged it in and tried it on a shirt. I don't know yet if I'm ready for that much satisfaction and independence.

A Fish to Write About

Something I've always wanted to do is write a piece for the paper about catching a big fish, the way the outdoor writers do.

I've been holding off for years, waiting on one thing: I needed to catch a big fish to write about. Finally last weekend I caught a black bass weighing four pounds. I decided that was big enough. The bass came out of a private lake owned by Helen and John Stockton who live in San Jacinto County a few miles out of Cleveland. When John saw my bass, he said it "was about three pounds." I thought it weighed closer to four. With a little coaching, I got Helen to say the fish looked to her like a solid four-pounder. We had no scales. So I sided with Helen, and my bass became a four-pounder by a split decision.

To outdoor writers, a bass weighing four pounds is

not worth a whole story, but to me it is. Because I've caught mostly miniature fish lately. For about the past year I've been trying to learn fly-fishing, and the biggest thing I've hooked on a fly rod would've been all right for trotline bait.

The Stocktons' lake covers only a few acres, but it has some big bass. Early and late, you can hear one of those heavyweights turning somersaults up in the shallows, and it sounds like somebody dropping a ham into a washpot.

I was in the lake's upper end, where a finger of water leads into a tree-lined cove. The water was calm. Its color just right. Clear but not too.

I'd borrowed John's bass boat. No, no, not one of those seventeen-foot vessels with forty horses on the back. This is simply two pontoons hooked together by a carpeted deck maybe five feet square. It has nice curved-back swivel seats and a troll motor that operates off a car battery, and it's wonderful for small lakes where you don't need to go fast.

Okay, the sun was getting low, and I was sitting back real comfortable, anchored in that cove where I could cast to the bank all around me. On my right I had my little ice chest, and I had a can of cold soda pop open down next to my foot. The bullfrogs were singing to me, and I didn't much care whether I caught anything or not.

I was throwing this purple worm, rigged weedless with the point of the hook buried just beneath the skin, the way they fix 'em in snaggy water. I had twelve-pound mono line on an open-faced spinning reel and a one-eighth-ounce bullet weight above the worm. (I have to put all this stuff in because the fishermen demand details.)

I've caught fish on plastic worms before. Not very good ones, though, and I don't really enjoy throwing worms. But John said worms, and it's his lake. He also said: "Work the lily pads. Try to make the worm land on a pad. Then drag it off slow, and let it sink. When you feel a tug, set the hook hard. I mean hard."

The first few tugs turned out to be the stems of lily pads, which are springy and truly tough. So I was hung on another stem, and I was yanking to get free, and the stem began circling off to my left, and the pad didn't go with it.

Because it wasn't a lily stem. It was this bass.

I couldn't reel in any line. I had the drag on that reel at a pessimistic setting, way too light. The fish kept stripping line. I put an awkward twist on the drag control. Twisted it too far, and for a few seconds I thought the bass would either break the line or take the rod out of my hand.

The strength a black bass this size can exert against light tackle is really extraordinary. I'm not sure I would ever catch enough fish to get accustomed to feeling that fury, that power born of desperation.

It circled the boat. It went beneath me twice and bent a third of the rod against the curve of the pontoon. Once it wrapped around the anchor line, and I figured, well, goodbye fish. But here came a miracle and unwrapped the mono, and I was still in business.

There was a stage in the catching of this fish when I was glad you weren't there to see me. It had grown tired and let me reel it close so I could lean forward to hook its lower lip with the thumb and hoist it in.

That's when my glasses fell out of my shirt pocket and came near going in the drink. My left foot kicked over the can of soda water, and it foamed onto my spectacles on the deck. My right foot upset the open tackle box, and here came its contents—Little Joes and Sprites and Rogues and Jigs and leaders and hooks and weights, scattering in a triple-hooked mess around my sneakers.

Even so, the bass didn't get away. When things quit rattling on the deck, I looked back at the water, and there was the bass, temporarily exhausted, waiting to come aboard.

When finally I got my fist in its mouth, I sat back and

put the fish in my lap and waited for my pulse rate to descend into safe numbers. The deck looked like a used battlefield. That bass cost me. I'm missing about ten dollars worth of lures that went in the water, I guess, when the tackle box spilled.

You want to know what I almost did? I almost turned it loose. It was so beautiful, and fat, and balanced. For a moment I thought it would be a good thing to do, just set it free.

But I couldn't bear not to show it. We cooked and ate it. It was wonderful, too. Still, I wish now I'd put it back. That would have made a better story.

◆————————————————————◆

Certified by the Government

A nurse I know gave me a stern lecture the other day. She works for one of the doctors I support. I have—let's see—five doctors who depend for a living on my physical curiosities. Some guys have lawyers. Some have stockbrokers. Some have accountants. Some have mistresses. Me, I have doctors.

What the nurse lectured me about was Medicare. She said I needed to get my Medicare card because I was already a year late. She told me where to go for it, and where you go is a Social Security office. Several of them around town.

So, finally I was sitting in one of the offices, filling out the form they gave me and waiting for my name to be called, when suddenly this great wave of wonder came rolling over me. And I heard my own voice speaking to me as follows:

"Hey, guess what? Guess who this is, sitting in here among all those other wrinkled and gray-haired people?

Well, it's *you*, that's who. You know what it means? It means that you are now recognized by the federal government as being officially *old*."

You care to hear how I feel about that? Well, I feel miscellaneous.

That's how Buck Thomas used to express it. He was a truck driver out at San Angelo. I worked for him as a swamper the summer I was twenty-one, and when he had conflicting notions about a matter, he always said he felt miscellaneous. Since that summer I have felt miscellaneous about a thousand questions, and getting old is among them.

When I was about forty I didn't care anything about getting old, and in fact I was close to being opposed to it. Old age seemed to have so many drawbacks, I had about decided it would be all right just to skip it.

But gradually I notice I've grown more interested in becoming an old, old man, and some days I dwell on it, and talk about it too much, and this causes my friends and some of the customers to fuss at me. Like here'll come a note from one of the customers who's eighty-seven, or some such beautiful age, laughing at me a little for feeling old.

Some days I do feel ancient as mountains, and now that I have been recorded by the federal government as an Old Dude, purebred and registered, maybe it's all right for me to talk about it now and then.

The best thing about getting this old is that people are generally kinder to me than they used to be. I need being kind to. It's among my necessities, and may even be the main one.

Another advantage is, being in the middle sixties gives you a reason to dismiss mysterious pains and not worry about them. This is a really profitable feature of aging.

Just since I sat down here to begin this report, I have experienced a nice example of this benefit. I had a sort of wandering pain. It began somewhere south. I couldn't lo-cate the source exactly. It meandered up my thigh, and glanced off my lower spine, and disbursed in my rib cage, like a tropical storm blowing itself out against mountains. It wasn't severe.

But if I'd had such a pain when I was forty, it would have scared the liver out of me. Probably I wouldn't have run to the doctor about it, though. Instead, I would have added it to my list of worries and imagined that it was a symptom of some dreadful disease that would kill me be-fore my kids were grown.

But now I simply say, no, it's only a part of getting old, and I may never have that kind of pain again. And prob-ably I won't. It's a relief, being in the position to blame every little ache on nothing but aging.

Something I do regret, in a way, about becoming a Medicare card carrier is that I've stopped yearning so in-tensely for what I don't have. Places I'd like to go. Things I can't do.

I haven't stopped yearning altogether, but I've gradu-ally slowed down, so that it doesn't hurt as much as it did. For forty years I felt that if I just kept hustling, kept on keeping on, then eventually something wonderful would happen and my life would become suddenly pretty close to perfect and I would go floating around the rest of my time on a pink satin cloud.

I see now that's not going to happen, or at least it isn't likely. I haven't given up hope, but I've quit pressing. In one way I miss the pressing, even though I'm glad to be rid of it. A little like old Buck Thomas, I feel miscellaneous about it.

Following are the dates of the issues of the *Houston Chronicle* in which the columns in this book first appeared: